NEWS DESERTS AND GHOST NEWSPAPERS:
WILL LOCAL NEWS SURVIVE?

By Penelope Muse Abernathy
Knight Chair in Journalism and Digital Media Economics

The Center for Innovation and Sustainability in Local Media
Hussman School of Journalism and Media

University of North Carolina at Chapel Hill

Distributed by the University of North Carolina Press
116 South Boundary Street
Chapel Hill, NC 27514-3808
uncpress.org

TABLE OF CONTENTS

PREFACE

The paradox of the coronavirus pandemic and the ensuing economic shutdown is that it has exposed the deep fissures that have stealthily undermined the health of local journalism in recent years, while also reminding us of how important timely and credible local news and information are to our health and that of our community.

This is a watershed year, and the choices we make in 2020 – as citizens, policymakers and industry leaders – will determine the future of the local news landscape. Will our actions – or inactions – lead to an "extinction-level event" of local newspapers and other struggling news outlets, as predicted by some in the profession? Or will they lead to a reset: an acknowledgment of what is at stake if we lose local news, as well as a recommitment to the civic mission of journalism and a determination to support its renewal?

In only a few months, the pandemic and the ensuing recession have greatly accelerated the loss of local news that has been occurring over the past two decades. Layoffs, pay cuts and furloughs have affected thousands of journalists in 2020. Dozens of newspapers have been closed, and there is the threat of dozens – even hundreds – more closures before year's end. While we don't yet know what the news landscape will look like in a post-pandemic world, we do know there will be a "new normal." Because this is a pivotal moment, now seems an appropriate time to hit pause and document the state of local news today. That way, we can begin to address the underlying structural issues that have contributed to the rise of news deserts.

This report is the fourth on the state of local news produced by the Hussman School of Journalism and Media at the University of North Carolina at Chapel Hill. It measures what has been lost, while also assessing what must be done if we are to nurture and revive a vibrant news landscape in the third decade of the 21st century.

The first section of this report, "The News Landscape in 2020: Transformed and Diminished," examines the loss of local news, from the end of 2004 – when newspaper advertising, circulation and employment were at, or near, peak levels – to the end of 2019, providing a time-lapsed snapshot of the news landscape before the coronavirus seized control of the economy. It assesses not only the current state of local newspapers, but also that of local digital sites, ethnic news organizations and public broadcasting outlets. The second section, "The News Landscape of the Future: Transformed . . . and Renewed?" establishes the need for a reimagining of journalistic, business, technological and policy solutions.

Extensive research has established that the loss of local news has significant political, social and economic implications for our democracy and our society. Yet, according to the Pew Research Center, almost three-quarters of the general public remain unaware of the dire economic situation confronting local news organizations. By documenting the transformation of the local news landscape over the past 15 years, and exploring the challenges and potential solutions, we hope this report will raise awareness of the role that all of us can play in supporting the revival of local news.

Accompanying this report, our updated website, usnewsdeserts.com – with more than 350 interactive maps – allows you to drill down to the county level to understand the state of local media in communities throughout the United States. You will find information on regional and community newspapers – as well as public broadcasting outlets, ethnic media and digital sites.

New this year, in both our report and prominently displayed on our website, we provide a quick exercise that allows you to assess the quality of local news in your community. We hope you will share this information with others and use it to support news organizations that take their civic mission seriously – whether they are digital sites, newspapers or broadcast outlets.

All of us have a stake in nurturing a strong local news environment. This includes the venture capitalists who fund start-ups, the hedge funds and private equity firms that invest in and own our news organizations, the tech companies that disseminate news and information, the government officials who craft policies, and the directors of corporate boards and philanthropic organizations that fund our local institutions. But, most of all, we as residents of the thousands of communities – large and small – that dot this vast country need reliable news and information to make wise decisions about issues that will affect the quality of our everyday lives and those of future generations.

THE NEWS LANDSCAPE 2020: TRANSFORMED AND DIMINISHED

In only two decades, successive technological and economic assaults have destroyed the for-profit business model that sustained local journalism in this country for two centuries. Hundreds of news organizations – century-old newspapers as well as nascent digital sites – have vanished. By early 2020, many survivors were hanging on by the slimmest of profit margins. Then, the coronavirus hit.

We can measure the loss of local news in recent years in two ways: the loss of newspapers and the loss of journalists. In the 15 years leading up to 2020, more than one-fourth of the country's newspapers disappeared, leaving residents in thousands of communities – inner-city neighborhoods, suburban towns and rural villages – living in vast news deserts. Simultaneously, half of all local journalists disappeared, as round after round of layoffs have left many surviving papers – the gutsy dailies and weeklies that had won accolades and Pulitzer Prizes for their reporting – mere "ghosts," or shells of their former selves. Compounding the problem, there has been a lack of capital and funding available to support a variety of for-profit, nonprofit and publicly funded news organizations attempting to thwart the rise of news deserts.

This is the fourth report by the UNC Hussman School of Journalism and Media, documenting and analyzing the loss of local news and its implications for our democracy. In the years immediately following the 2008 recession, the decline has been relentless, and it appears to have been accelerating in the years leading up to 2020. Since our last report, "The Expanding News Desert," was published in the fall of 2018:

- 300 newspapers closed, another 6,000 journalists employed by newspapers vanished, and print newspaper circulation declined by 5 million.

- Consolidation also increased, with the largest chains, backed by private equity firms and hedge funds, racing to merge with the last surviving publicly traded companies and form mega-chains with hundreds of newspapers, and management focused on shareholder return over journalism's civic duty.

- Despite the efforts of other media, including commercial television and digital sites, to step into the breach, they have failed to thwart the rise of news deserts, especially in economically struggling regions of the country. Independent digital sites, once seen as potential saviors, are failing to achieve long-term financial security. While more than 80 local online sites were established in 2019, an equal number went dark.

Since then, the economic fallout from the coronavirus has turbo-charged the decline – with at least 30 newspapers closed or merged in April and May 2020, dozens of newspapers switching to online-only delivery of news, and thousands of journalists at legacy and digital news operations being furloughed or laid off.[1] All of this raises anew fears of an "extinction-level event" that destroys many of the survivors and newcomers, and leads to the collapse of the country's local news ecosystem.[2]

Even before the coronavirus crisis, it was apparent that the local news ecosystem was in peril, journalistically and economically.[3] Some of the harm has been self-inflicted. An initial lethargy, or arrogance, at many newspapers hindered innovation and a quick response to a rapidly shifting environment. As the industry went into free fall, many newspaper owners also adopted the business practices introduced by the large private equity and hedge fund owners that prioritized bottom-line performance over journalism's civic mission, dooming hundreds of news organizations to irrelevance. And there was a failure by both legacy news organizations, as well as digital start-ups, to use the new technology to reach out and engage audiences in new, more relevant ways and give voice to the voiceless, the disenfranchised – ethnic, poor and less educated – communities in the country.

However, much of the decline was inevitable, as the business model collapsed for news organizations and a viable substitute digital model has so far failed to emerge. There was an initial naiveté about the possibilities of the digital age that blinded policymakers, the industry and news consumers to the unintended political, economic and social consequences. Instead, the intrusive, always-on internet swiftly siphoned off readers, advertisers and profits. With Facebook and Google capturing the vast majority of digital revenue in many communities today, traditional news organizations, as well as online outlets, have been reduced to fighting over the digital scraps. The long-lasting recession of 2008 further weakened many news organizations – especially those in economically distressed communities, where many local businesses filed for bankruptcy and unemployment remained high, even as the stock market rallied. Without increased funding to support for-profit, nonprofit and publicly funded news enterprises, digital start-ups – as well as newspapers, public and commercial broadcasting outlets and ethnic media – have struggled to attain the strong financial footing necessary to experiment with and develop new business models that will allow them to adequately address the local news deficit.

This first section in the 2020 report, divided into four chapters, examines the state of local news, from the end of 2004 to the end of 2019. It provides a snapshot of the local news landscape in the moments before the coronavirus struck:

Vanishing Newspapers

Over the past 15 years, the United States has lost 2,100 newspapers, leaving at least 1,800 communities that had a local news outlet in 2004 without any at the beginning of 2020. To date, most of losses were weeklies in economically struggling communities. However, two closings in the past year – The Vindicator, a daily in the Ohio city of Youngstown, and The Sentinel, a weekly in the Maryland suburbs of Washington, D.C. – were especially notable: Youngstown, Ohio, became the first city of any size in the country to lose its sole surviving daily newspaper, and the closing of The Sentinel, a small weekly, improbably left the 1 million residents of Maryland's affluent Montgomery County without a local newspaper.

Vanishing Readers and Journalists

Half of newspaper readers and journalists have also vanished over the past 15 years. Many of the country's 6,700 surviving papers have become "ghost newspapers" – mere shells of their former selves, with greatly diminished newsrooms and readership. The loss of both journalists and circulation speaks to the declining influence of local newspapers, and raises questions about their long-term financial viability in a digital era.

The New Media Giants

Despite the shrinking universe of surviving papers, the chains are bigger than ever – and, poised to grow even bigger, with the creation of a handful of highly leveraged mega-chains formed by the union of large publicly traded newspaper companies with large hedge funds and private equity firms. Massive consolidation in the newspaper industry has shifted editorial and business decisions to a few large corporations without strong ties to the communities where their papers are located. As profitability has superseded journalism's civic mission on many newspapers, trust in local media has declined.

Entrepreneurial Stalwarts and Start-ups

A variety of legacy and start-up news outlets are currently attempting to fill the local news void. This year, UNC researchers examined the state of the country's 525 online news outlets, 950 ethnic media and 1,400 public broadcasting stations. Their pioneering efforts hold promise, but the challenge is finding a way to scale their efforts. There is a critical need for more funding of for-profit, nonprofit and publicly funded business models.

Economists define journalism as a "public good"[4] because the information in news stories informs wise decisions about important issues that can affect the quality of life of the nation's 330 million residents. In the absence of a local news organization, social media and internet sites often have become the default media for reading, viewing and sharing news – as well as rumor and gossip – exacerbating political, social and economic divisions in a polarized nation.[5]

The virus has focused the attention of many in society – policymakers, as well as ordinary citizens – on what is at risk when we lose the news. Among the existential questions that need to be answered in the months ahead as news organizations attempt to recover from the coronavirus devastation: Who produces local news in the digital age? How will local news be delivered? Who has access to it? Who pays for the news we consume?

But before we can look ahead, we need to first understand how we got to this point and what we have learned so far.

The findings in this report are based on analysis of data collected by the Hussman School of Journalism and Media at the University of North Carolina at Chapel Hill over the past five years. Our study attempts to measure the loss of news through quantitative and qualitative research. It seeks to answer this question: Are residents in a community getting credible news that helps them make informed decisions about quality-of-life issues? In addition to newspapers, we've collected information on local independent news sites, ethnic news organizations and public broadcasting outlets. You can learn more about the state of news in your community by visiting our website, usnewsdeserts.com, which allows you to drill down to the county level in every state, using our 400 national and state interactive maps.

This is our fourth report. Three previous reports, the most recent being "The Expanding News Desert" (2018), have chronicled the rise of a new media baron, the emergence of local news deserts and various attempts by alternative media to fill the local news void. Two books, "Saving Community Journalism: The Path to Profitability (2014)" and "The Strategic Digital Media Entrepreneur (2018)," explored the potential for local news organizations to transform themselves and develop sustainable business models.

VANISHING NEWSPAPERS

Key Takeaways

1. Since 2004, the United States has lost one-fourth – 2,100 – of its newspapers. This includes 70 dailies and more than 2,000 weeklies or nondailies.

2. At end of 2019, the United States had 6,700 newspapers, down from almost 9,000 in 2004.

3. Today, more than 200 of the nation's 3,143 counties and equivalents have no newspaper and no alternative source of credible and comprehensive information on critical issues. Half of the counties have only one newspaper, and two-thirds do not have a daily newspaper.

4. Many communities that lost newspapers were the most vulnerable – struggling economically and isolated.

When the 127-year-old Siftings Herald in Arkadelphia, Arkansas, printed its final edition on Sept. 15, 2018, there were only 1,600 subscribers in a community of 10,000 residents.[6] The community was one of the poorest in the state. For decades, the paper had been published daily, Monday through Friday. But as both subscriber and advertising revenue dropped, publication was first reduced to two days a week in 2016, and then in early September 2018, the owner, the Gatehouse chain, announced the simultaneous closure of the Siftings Herald and two other papers in nearby counties. A former editor, now a columnist at the Democrat-Gazette in Little Rock, took note of the closures, writing, "The watchdogs of school boards, city councils and quorum courts are gone. The chroniclers of high school sports teams are missing. To say that this is a sad thing for these counties is to understate the case."[7]

For more than two centuries, newspaper editors and reporters, more often than not, served as arbiters of our news, determining what made front-page headlines read by millions of people in this country. They were the prime, if not sole, source of credible and comprehensive news and information, especially for residents in small and mid-sized communities.[8]

Researchers in disciplines such as political science, sociology and economics have identified three ways strong local newspapers historically built a sense of community and trust in our democracy. Through their journalism, they set the agenda for debate of important public policy issues, and, as a result, influenced the course of history with the stories they published and their editorials that recommended specific actions. Their advertising encouraged regional economic growth and development by helping local businesses connect with local consumers. Newspapers also nurtured social cohesion and political participation by putting into local context issues that may have seemed to be national ones, such as health care or gun control.[9]

According to several estimates, as much as 85 percent of the news that feeds our democracy originates with newspapers.[10] Since local newspapers have historically been equal parts business enterprises and civic institutions, the collapse of the for-profit business model that sustained newspapers until recently has also placed in jeopardy the journalistic mission.

From revolutionary days to the early 20th century, newspapers flourished in our country. As pioneers moved West in the 19th century, one of the first orders of business – right after hiring a lawman to keep order – was establishing a local newspaper. A newspaper gave a sense of time and place to the first settlers, and helped residents connect with one another as dusty crossroads grew into real communities. The number of newspapers peaked in the early 1900s, when there were an estimated 24,000 weekly and daily publications, with two in five newspapers located in communities west of the Mississippi.[11] Even small and mid-sized communities had two newspapers. But as the popularity of television surged in the years after World War II, afternoon papers fell by the wayside, leaving most communities with only one surviving newspaper – either a daily or a weekly.

By 2004, there were only 9,000 papers still publishing. Since then, the United States has lost one-fourth – or 2,100 – of its newspapers. In the country today, there are 6,730 surviving papers, including 1,260 dailies (published four or more times a week) and 5,470 nondailies or weeklies. The three-fourths of newspapers in this country have circulations under 15,000.

About 1,800 of the communities that have lost a paper since 2004 do not have easy access to any local news scource – such as a local online news site or a local radio station.[12]

It is useful to think of the country's newspaper ecosystem as a pyramid, with a very large base of small papers serving communities ranging in size from a few hundred to a million or more residents.[13] The 6,570 papers that form the base

THE LOCAL NEWS ECOSYSTEM

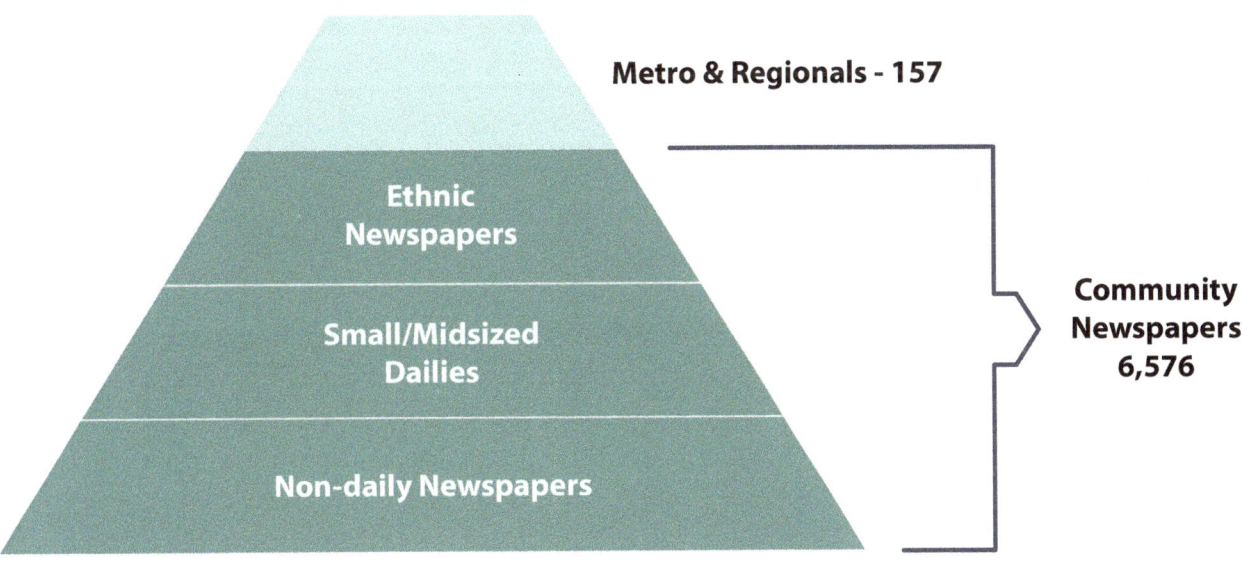

include small dailies, as well as weeklies and ethnic newspapers. They help residents in small and mid-sized communities understand what is going on in their community and also put into local context national issues such as the opioid crisis or the coronavirus pandemic. In other words, these small local newspapers help residents in a community understand what interests they share with their next-door neighbors and the best of them mobilize grassroots efforts to address local issues. They also connect local businesses with consumers through their advertising.

The 150 or so surviving regional papers in the country bind a metro area or a state together. They have historically provided the majority of investigative and analytical reporting that prompts both local, state – and even national – government officials to enact major policies that address the problems. The journalists at these papers spot trends among the various smaller community papers, and their reporters on beats, such as education, health and politics, provided journalistic oversight and editorial commentary on areas that affect the future of all residents in a city, region or state. In other words, the journalism in these metro and regional dailies connects residents of communities in one area of a state with those in a distant part of the state, helping them come together to solve statewide problems.

At the very top of the pyramid are the three national newspapers – The New York Times, Wall Street Journal and USA Today – with circulation and online readership in excess of several million. The national papers are excluded from this analysis of the local news landscape since they have a journalistic mandate and a business model, which rely on scale and reach, that are very different from that of either the state and metro papers or smaller community papers.[14]

National and state papers have historically relied heavily on journalism done at small local papers to initially report on events and decisions that later become state and national headlines. Hometown papers not only record the history of their communities – the ebb and flow of daily life – they can also change the course of history by reporting on a shooting or a local protest. The larger papers then amplify the initial work done by the small newspaper. But as hometown papers disappear – and the state and regional papers lay off veteran journalists and pull back on coverage and circulation in outlying communities – the news ecosystem is imperiled.

THE VANISHING DAILIES

In July 2019, the longtime family owners of The Vindicator in Youngstown, Ohio, announced they were shuttering the 150-year-old newspaper at the end of August after failing to find a buyer. When journalists on the paper learned this, they gathered in Managing Editor Mark Sweetwood's office. He called on them to remember the paper's crusading legacy and encouraged them, "To the last minute to the last hour of the last day, we are giving this thing a Viking funeral. We can't change the circumstances, but we are going to walk out of here with our heads held high."[15]

At its demise, The Vindicator, which employed more than 30 journalists, had a circulation of only 35,000, serving a metropolitan area of half a million residents, where a third are living in poverty. The Vindicator's closing made national headlines and caused much angst in the industry as Youngstown became the first city of any size in the country to lose its sole surviving daily newspaper. Could this be a harbinger of what was to befall daily newspapers in other large metro areas?

Since 2004, 70 dailies have vanished from the U.S. landscape, and most of those have been papers serving small and mid-sized communities. Only four of the shuttered dailies had circulations above 100,000 when they closed, and all four were located in two-newspaper cities – the Rocky Mountain News in Denver, the Seattle Post/Intelligencer, the Honolulu Star-Bulletin, and the Tampa Tribune. Today, there are only a handful of metro areas – most notably, New York, Washington, Chicago and Los Angeles – that still have two or more daily newspapers.

The vast majority of the dailies that closed in recent years served impoverished communities that never regained their economic footing in the years after the 2008 recession.[16] Many of these dailies lost not only their local advertisers, who went out of business in the wake of the recession, but also their readers, who could no longer afford to pay for a subscription. When they closed their doors, most of the shuttered dailies had less than 15,000 print subscribers, even though they served communities with tens of thousands of residents. After two deals to sell the family-owned Waycross Journal-Herald fell through, the longtime publisher, Roger Williams, told employees that the six-day-a-week daily would publish its final edition on Sept. 30, 2019. At its closing, the small daily paper, with a circulation of only 6,700, was distributed in three Georgia counties, where more than one in five residents lived in poverty. With declining subscription and advertising revenue, "we didn't have any recourse," Williams said.[17] Two weeks after the closure of the Waycross Journal-Herald, the owner of The Brantley Beacon in Nahunta, 23 miles away, announced he planned to resume publishing the Journal-Herald, but as a weekly.[18]

As advertisers and readers abandoned the daily paper, the owners – both large chains and independent publishers – often tried to stave off closing of the newspaper by switching from daily to nondaily printing of the paper. About a tenth of the more than 2,000 weeklies shuttered over the past 15 years were listed as dailies in the 2004 UNC database. Most had been published daily for decades. The 127-year-old Siftings Herald in Arkansas switched to twice-weekly in 2016, three years before its demise.[19] The Daily Times of Pryor Creek in Oklahoma, established in 1919, switched to publishing only three times a week in 2013. When The Pryor Creek Times published its last issue as a thrice-weekly on April 29, 2017, it had only 3,000 subscribers among the 40,000 residents of Mayes County.[20]

Other owners of dailies took more drastic steps and stopped the printing presses entirely. More than 100 papers (including at least a dozen of the daily newspapers) that were printed and distributed in 2004 are now online-only sites. Over time, these slimmed-down websites have either withered in terms of impact and reach, or they have been absorbed into the website of a surviving paper. In 2009, the Seattle Post-Intelligencer switched to digital-only publication. In 2018, its website was placed under the umbrella of the San Francisco Chronicle's free website, SFGate. More recently, in 2017, The News-Sentinel in Fort Wayne, Indiana, ceased daily publication and became a website. In 2018, seven of the eight remaining employees of the News-Sentinel digital site were laid off.[21]

TOTAL NUMBER OF U.S. NEWSPAPERS: 2004 & 2020

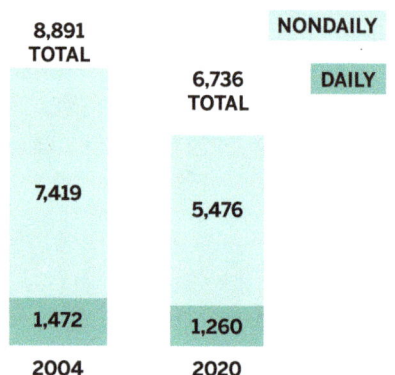

There has been a net loss of 2,155 papers since 2004.

This net loss takes into account more than 100 dailies that shifted to weekly publication, as well as several dozen new weeklies that were established during that period. In total, 71 dailies and 2,196 weeklies closed or merged with other papers.

Source: UNC Database

When a community loses its daily, residents are usually reliant on news outlets in adjacent or faraway counties for coverage, since there are few local alternatives. In the aftermath of the closure of the Vindicator, several news organizations attempted to fill the void. The Ogden chain, which owns the newspaper in the adjacent county of Trumball, purchased the Vindicator's subscription list and its front-page nameplate, and in fall 2019 began publishing a zoned edition with limited news. The Youngstown Business Journal started beefing up its coverage of topics, including entertainment.[22] And the McClatchy chain, in partnership with the Google News Initiative, established MahoningMatters, designed to explore "potential sustainable business models for local news" in Mahoning County. However, the site employs only three of the 30 journalists working at The Vindicator when it closed.[23]

Despite the new additions, Mark Brown, general manager of The Vindicator and son of the longtime publisher and owner, believes something important is lost by not having a paper with ties to the community that endured for 150 years. He hopes people remember how hard his family fought to preserve crusading journalism in Mahoning Valley, going to court to get access to public records, often sending the paper's attorney with its journalists to meetings to make certain the politicians were following open meeting laws. "We fought those battles like crazy," he said. "I'm very concerned that is what's lost."[24]

THE VANISHING WEEKLIES

Residents of the Kentucky community of Morehead awoke on the morning of April 29, 2020, to learn they had joined a growing number of university towns – from Chapel Hill, North Carolina, to Baldwin City, Kansas – with the dubious distinction of having lost their weekly newspaper. Citing the loss of advertising revenue due to the coronavirus pandemic, Community Newspapers Holding Inc. (CNHI), announced that The Morehead News – and four other weeklies the chain owned in northeastern Kentucky – would be merged with The Daily Independent in Ashland, 55 miles away.[25]

"Many dailies have swallowed up sister weeklies, but it's unusual if not unprecedented for such a consolidation over such a distance," wrote Al Cross, director of the Institute for Rural Journalism and Community Issues at the University of Kentucky. "It dismayed people in Morehead, home to Morehead State University, [because of] some recent economic developments, including a huge complex of greenhouses intended to provide vegetables to the Eastern United States." A former spokesman for MSU told Cross that a local economic development official had observed, "I can't say to a prospect, we've got everything you want in a small town, except a newspaper. ... If you don't have a newspaper in your community, how backward are you?"[26] In addition to the five weeklies in Kentucky, CNHI, which is owned by the state-pension fund of Alabama, closed seven other weeklies across the Midwest and South.[27]

Weekly and nondaily papers often have an outsized impact on their communities, but in contrast to the dailies, their closing rarely makes headlines outside the community where they are located. More than 2,000 weeklies and nondaily papers have been shuttered since 2004. Most had circulation of less than 8,000 when they failed.

Two-thirds of nondaily newspapers closed since 2004 are located in metro areas, leaving a vacuum for residents of America's urban neighborhoods and suburbs, who

WHERE HAVE NEWSPAPERS DISAPPEARED?

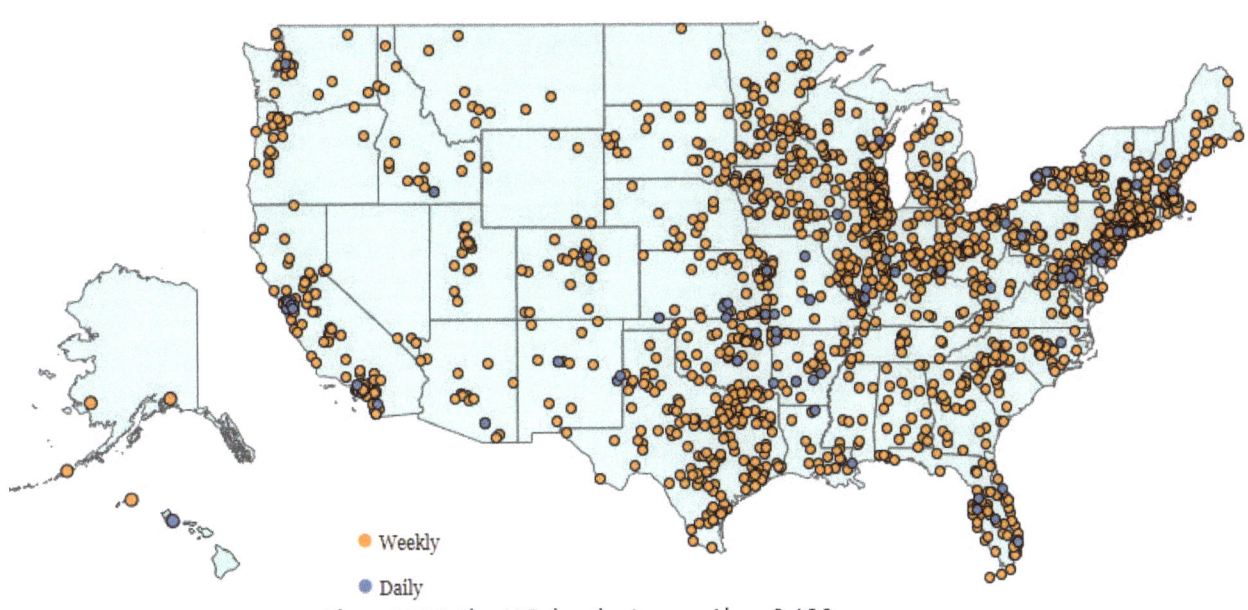

● Weekly

● Daily

Since 2004, the U.S. has lost more than 2,100 newspapers.

Source: UNC Hussman School of Journalism and Media

typically relied on the local paper to keep them informed about everything from municipal candidates to property assessments and real-estate transactions. Many of the shuttered city and suburban weeklies were owned by some of the largest newspaper chains, such as Gatehouse and Digital First. The decision to shut them down – or merge them with other weeklies or dailies – is often made by executives who opt to deploy their financial resources and journalistic focus elsewhere. In 2013, the CEO of Gatehouse told the Boston Globe that corporate decisions about when to close or consolidate weeklies depended – not on the journalistic mission – but on the economic viability of the markets where the papers were located. "We're going to shift resources to the highest potential markets that are most desirable to our advertisers," he said.[28] The company has periodically pruned its Boston area portfolio, which included more than 100 weeklies in 2010. As it prepared to acquire the Gannett chain in 2019, Gatehouse merged 32 of its remaining 50 weeklies in the Boston area suburbs into only 18 publications.[29]

In 2015, The Washington Post abruptly closed all 20 of its Maryland weeklies in affluent Montgomery County, shortly after Jeff Bezos, who had purchased The Post, failed to find a buyer. Bezos had decided to focus all his resources on positioning The Washington Post as a national paper. The papers, collectively known as The Gazette, had a free circulation of 450,000.[30]

The closure of The Gazette meant that a family-owned weekly, the 165-year-old Montgomery Sentinel, was the only local newspaper covering a county of more than 1 million residents. But, in January 2020, publisher Lynn Kapiloff announced that the Sentinel was closing. Having lost almost all of the local display and classified advertising it carried in the 1990s, the Sentinel was left with only legal advertising, which didn't cover the costs of producing the paper and paying the staff.[31] At its peak in the 1990s, the Sentinel had a circulation of more than 100,000. By 2020, the weekly had a circulation in Montgomery County of only 5,000. County Council member Nancy Navarro worried about the lack of news coverage of local government. After the demise of the Gazette, "We barely have any (local coverage)," she said, "and overall, this is bad for our democracy."[32]

The struggles of The Sentinel are typical of those confronting many owners of locally owned weeklies today. Weeklies are not as capital intensive as dailies, and, as a result, it is much easier for someone to find the funds to publish a neighborhood newsletter or paper. However, weeklies are also much more susceptible to downturns in the local market. In contrast to the dailies, weeklies typically employ a very small staff – maybe no more than a couple of people, who handle both the business and journalism. So, there is no room to pare back when times are hard.

While both low-income and affluent neighborhoods in metro areas have lost their hometown papers, most of the shuttered 600 weeklies in rural areas were located in small markets with high poverty rates. Most had an average circulation of less than 4,000, underscoring the small size of their communities. Newspaper publishers found it difficult to attract paying customers, as well as advertising from businesses in the area.

When Gatehouse announced that the 130-year-old Carthage Press in Southwest Missouri would print its final edition August 29, 2018, it had a circulation of only 1,200. Almost a third of the people in Carthage live in poverty. A group of local residents announced they would take over publication the following month, but they, too, were forced to close the paper by the end of 2019.[33]

LIVING IN A NEWS DESERT

The coronavirus has brought into sharp focus the critical role that a local news outlet can play during an epidemic or emergency – disseminating authoritative information from experts and discrediting misinformation. An analysis by the Brookings Institution found that in early April 2020, half of the 2,485 counties that reported cases of coronavirus had either no local newspaper or only one surviving paper. Fifty-seven percent of those counties in the country lacked a daily newspaper. Two-thirds were rural counties. It concluded, "Undoubtedly important stories will go uncovered as the coronavirus spreads across the country" – especially into rural areas, with poorer health care facilities than in metro areas and vulnerable populations that are at high risk of contracting the virus.[34]

What is a "news desert"? Both scholars and policymakers have tackled the question in recent years. Some have focused on the digital divide and sought to determine whether residents have readily available access to broadband and wireless technology. Others

focus on barriers, such as language and cultural issues, that leave ethnic communities marginalized and disenfranchised. Still others focus on the quality and quantity of news available.[35]

At the heart of the debate is the notion that all residents in a community need access to critical information in order to make wise decisions that will affect the quality of their lives. Therefore, this report defines a news desert as "a community, either rural or urban, where residents have very limited access to the sort of credible and comprehensive news and information that feed democracy at the grassroots level."

Local newspapers have historically employed many more reporters than television and radio, and even in their diminished state, still provide the majority of what the Federal Communications Commission terms "critical information" on topics such as education, health, politics, governance and infrastructure.[36] A recent study by Duke University of 100 mid-sized communities, ranging in

DO YOU LIVE IN A NEWS DESERT?

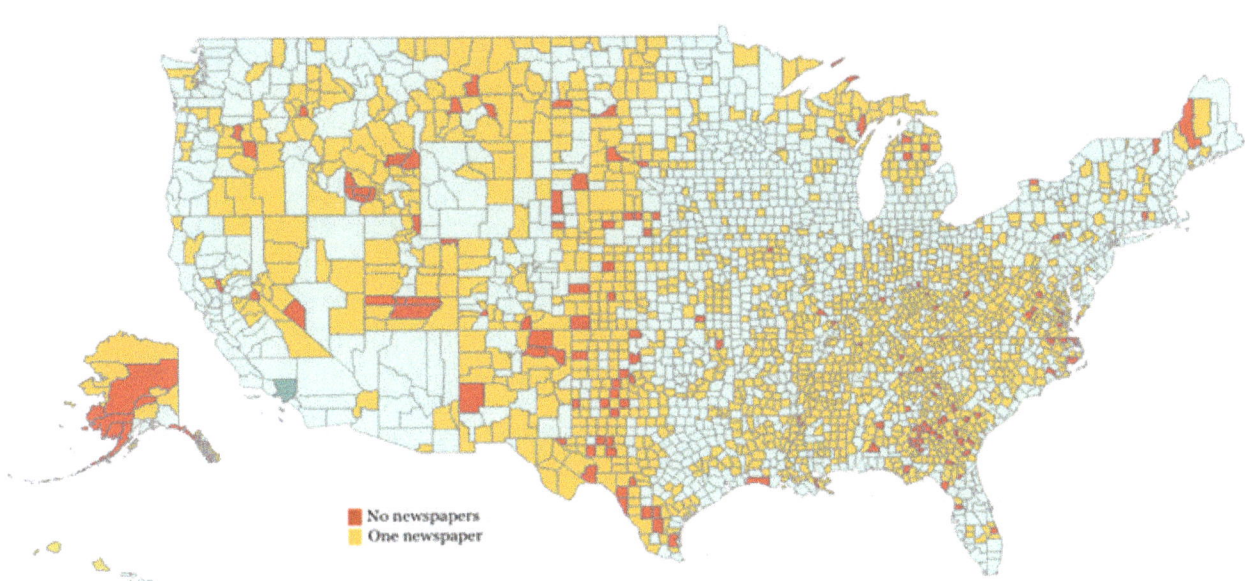

■ No newspapers
■ One newspaper

In the U.S. 200 counties do not have a local newspaper. Half of all counties - 1,540 - have only one newspaper, usually a weekly.

Source: UNC Hussman School of Journalism and Media

DEMOGRAPHIC PROFILES OF COUNTIES WITHOUT NEWSPAPERS

Demographic Measure	News Deserts	U.S.
Average Poverty Rate	18%	12%
Average Median Income ($/Year)	$45,000	$61,937
Average Median Age (Years)	42	38
Average Percent of Residents With Bachelor's Degree or Higher	19%	33%

Source: UNC Database and US Census Bureau

size from 20,000 to 300,000, found "local newspapers significantly outperformed local TV, radio, and online-only outlets in news production, both in overall story output and in terms of stories that are original, local, or address a critical information need."[37] This means that for many communities, the local paper is still the prime, if not the sole, source of news and information about topics such as local education and governance, as well as what is on sale at the grocery store.

Today, more than 200 of nation's 3,143 counties have no local newspaper. Half of the nation's counties – 1,540 – have only one newspaper. Additionally, two-thirds – 2,000 – no longer have a daily newspaper, which means residents in those counties typically turn to social media or regional television stations in distant cities for daily news.

News deserts are widespread and can occur in inner-city neighborhoods and suburban towns, as well as sparsely populated rural communities. Most communities that have lost a newspaper are struggling economically. They are slowly dying, bypassed by the technological revolution – the very communities where residents most need news and information on topics such as education, health and infrastructures. When a community loses its newspaper, coverage of routine local government

meetings almost always declines. Without a professional journalist covering those meetings, transparency and government efficiency also decline. Residents in those communities frequently end up paying higher taxes as the cost of government borrowing rises.[38]

Residents of counties with no newspaper – or only one newspaper – tend to be much poorer, older and less educated than the average American. Eighteen percent are living in poverty, compared with a national average of 12 percent. Almost half of residents living in a county without a newspaper also live in a food desert, "without access to fresh fruit, vegetables and other healthful whole foods."[39] They are less likely to be able to afford subscriptions to either cable or newspapers.[40] Many do not have access to high-speed internet in their homes or at work. As a result, residents of low-income areas tend to be overlooked by advertisers and have less access to print or digital media. Because they are less informed about key issues confronting their communities, they are less likely to vote.[41]

News deserts contribute to cultural, economic and political divides in this country, between media-rich communities typically located in metro areas and those in news-deprived regions, mostly located in the South and Midwest. The South, which has some of the poorest states in the country, has the most counties without newspapers. Every state in the South had at least one county without a newspaper. There were two dozen counties without a stand-alone newspaper in both Texas, with 254 counties, and Georgia, with 159. Several other states in the South, with many fewer counties – including Virginia, North Carolina and Tennessee – had at least a half-dozen counties without newspapers.[42]

No state has been spared the death of a newspaper. California has lost the most dailies, 11. They ranged from 22,000 to 157,000 in circulation. This loss was primarily driven by the merger of eight dailies, owned by the Digital First chain in the San Francisco Bay Area, into two nameplates, the East Bay Times and Mercury News. Illinois, New York and Texas – some of the nation's most populous states – lost the most weeklies, more than 150 each since 2004. Most of the weeklies closed in Illinois and New York were in the suburbs of metro areas. More than half of the weeklies in Texas were in rural areas.

States in the South, Midwest and Rocky Mountain regions were most likely to have counties with only one local newspaper. The sole surviving newspaper in those counties often covered vast geographic areas with populations ranging from a few hundred to several hundred thousand.

Ultimately, the loss of a local newspaper in one state has the potential to affect residents in other states. Government agencies often depend on local newspaper reports to help identify and contain public health crises, such as epidemics and pandemics.[43] "While online outlets of news and information have sprouted up everywhere ... few have been able to replace the reach and professional level of traditional news outlets," noted a researcher at New York University's School of Law, in a recent article about the threat that the rise of news deserts poses to national security, especially as the coronavirus affects the decisions of people living in even the most remote communities.[44]

COUNTIES WITHOUT NEWSPAPERS BY REGION: 2020

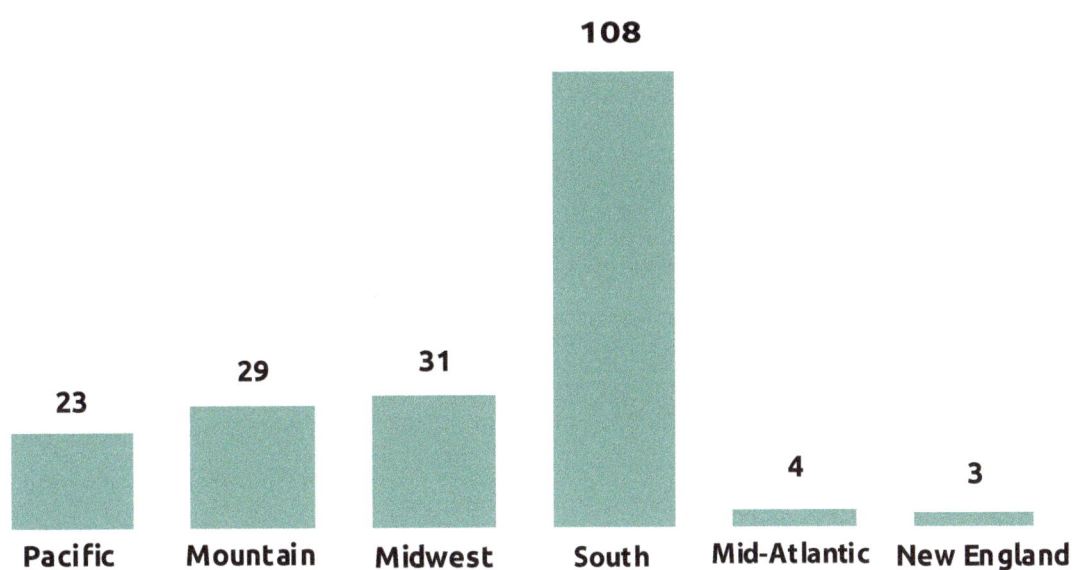

States were grouped into regions according to the following classifications: **Pacific**: AK, CA, HI, OR, WA; **Mountain**: AZ, CO, ID, MT, NV, NM, UT, WY; **Midwest**: IL, IN, MI, OH, WI, IA, KS, MN, MO, NE, ND, SD; **South**: DE, DC, FL, GA, MD, NC, SC, VA, WV, AL, KY, MS, TN, AR, LA, OK, TX; **Mid-Atlantic**: NJ, NY, PA; **New England**: CT, ME, MA, NH, RI, VT

SOURCE: UNC Database

VANISHING READERS AND JOURNALISTS

Key Takeaways

1. Half of newspaper readers and journalists have vanished over the past 15 years. Total circulation decreased by 55 million between 2004 and 2019. During the same period, newspapers lost 36,000 journalists.

2. The loss of both was driven by the collapse of the for-profit business model that sustained newspapers in the 20th century.

3. In response, publishers either closed unprofitable newspapers or relied on cost-cutting measures to retain profitability, eliminating print circulation, especially in outlying areas, and laying off journalists who cover the news. Metro and regional daily papers have been disproportionately responsible for the decline in journalists.

While a fourth of the country's newspapers have vanished since 2004, many of the 6,700 survivors have become "ghost newspapers" – mere shells of their former selves, with greatly diminished newsrooms and readership. Strategic decisions to close small weeklies and dailies, discontinue distribution of large dailies to outlying regions of the state, and lay off reporters contributed to the loss of almost half of print newspaper readers and journalists.

Between 2004 and 2019, total weekday circulation – including both dailies and weeklies – declined 45 percent, from more than 122 million to 68 million. Daily papers lost 22 million print readers. Only 39 dailies had a circulation of more than 100,000 in 2019, compared with 104 in 2004. Most of the drop in daily circulation resulted from decisions by owners of dailies to pare back distribution of the print paper, especially in outlying areas. The dramatic circulation drop occurred despite new rules adopted by the industry after 2004 that allowed newspapers to count print and online readership that had previously been excluded.[45] While online readership for most daily newspapers exceeds print readership, newspapers have struggled with getting readers to pay even a small amount for online access, a prerequisite for including those digital numbers in the industry-accepted audit of circulation conducted by the Alliance for Audited Media (AAM).

Circulation for weeklies declined from 72 million in 2014 to 40 million in 2019, and the decline was primarily the result of the closure of more than 2,000 weeklies or nondaily papers. The shuttered papers included large weeklies, such as The Gazette in the Maryland suburbs of Washington, D.C., which had a circulation of 450,000 when it was closed, as well as small papers, such as the Carthage Press in Missouri with 1,200 circulation. The average circulation of the country's surviving 5,500 weeklies and nondailies is 8,000. However, that probably overstates the actual paid subscription level of most weeklies and small dailies. Only 13 percent of papers in the UNC database subscribe to AAM audits. Many smaller newspapers – dailies, as well as weeklies – either self-report their circulation to sources such as Editor and Publisher, or don't share any statistics. The circulation figures for many of the nondailies and weeklies have been unchanged for over a decade. Most likely, many weeklies have supplemented declines in paid subscribers with free distribution in an effort to hold their circulation at a certain level.

At the same time newspapers were shedding readers, they were also shedding journalists. Between 2008 and 2018, the number of reporters and editors employed by newspapers dropped from 71,000 to 35,000.[46] The large regional dailies have shed the most journalists – an estimated 24,000 – or two-thirds of the total. Many large dailies, which often had several hundred journalists on staff in the late 1990s, today have only a few dozen.

The loss of both journalists and circulation speaks to the declining influence of state and regional newspapers, as well as the small community papers. Historically, journalists provided readers with transparency and insights into the decisions made by elected officials, and, in a mutually beneficial exchange, government officials relied on newspapers to get the word out to readers when there were important issues on the agenda.[47] With fewer journalists, there are fewer stories. And with fewer readers, the local newspaper ceases to be a community megaphone. A less-informed public is less likely to vote. Recent research has found that when a newspaper pulls back on circulation and coverage in a community, voter participation – especially in off-cycle elections – goes down.[48]

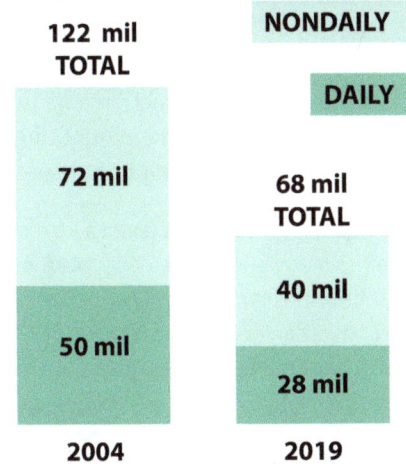

TOTAL U.S. CIRCULATION 2004 & 2019

122 mil TOTAL

NONDAILY

DAILY

72 mil

68 mil TOTAL

50 mil

40 mil

28 mil

2004

2019

Circulation has decreased 54 million since 2004.

The dramatic loss of readers and journalists also raises questions about the long-term financial viability of print newspapers in the digital era. The business model that sustained print regional and community newspapers in the 20th century relied on advertisers to provide 80 to 90 percent of the revenue. Local newspapers essentially purchased readers by offering subscriptions that covered only a fraction of the cost of gathering and producing the news, then turned around and sold their audiences at a premium to local advertisers, who wanted to reach people who lived in a certain geographic area. In the latter half of the 20th century, the sole surviving newspaper in many markets was often a de facto monopoly, able to set rates for both print advertisers and readers. As a result, papers in smaller markets often operated at 20 to 40 percent profit margins.[49]

But, by 2011, reader habits had shifted, with more people getting their news online than from a newspaper. Advertisers followed readers, causing the collapse of the print business model. Complicating matters, newspapers have had a very difficult time transitioning to digital business models since Facebook and Google receive a majority of all digital revenue in even the smallest markets.[50]

As advertising revenue and profit margins declined rapidly, the metro dailies tended to play a game of attrition, by reducing distribution of the print paper and laying off dozens, even hundreds, of their journalists. In contrast, the small dailies and weeklies, about a third of which are locally owned and operated, had much less ability to cut back since they had many fewer journalists – an average of fewer than five – and much smaller distribution footprints. When revenue dropped, they either accepted diminished profit margins or closed their business if they could not find a buyer. Whether daily or weekly, print advertising and circulation revenue still accounts for between half and three-quarters of most newspapers' total revenue. Going forward, however, the path to survival will most likely look very different for state and metro dailies versus smaller weeklies and nondailies.

WHERE HAVE ALL THE READERS GONE?

By the end of 2010, the number of people getting their news online surpassed those reading the local newspaper.[51] By the end of 2018, more people said they got their news from social media than print newspapers.[52] Did readers abandon print newspapers? Or did newspapers abandon their print readers?

Certainly, consumer preference played a key role. Getting news online has many advantages. The internet is always on, and, thanks to the technology that powers Google and Facebook, readers can quickly access news from multiple sources with just a few keystrokes. As if that wasn't enough incentive, most newspapers followed the lead of The New York Times, which did not charge for online access until 2011. So as high-speed internet became more prevalent, newspaper readers got used to getting their local news online for free – or next to nothing – on their mobile devices as well as their computers.

Corporate business decisions also played a role in accelerating the decline of print readership. As print advertising revenue began dropping rapidly, publishers and owners of the large metro and regional papers scrambled to simultaneously cut circulation costs while raising revenue. They pulled back on expensive distribution in outlying regions of the state and raised print subscription rates to compensate for advertising declines. Between 2004 to 2019, the yearly rate for a print subscription to many regional dailies tripled – from $150 to as much as $600. The actions of The Atlanta Journal-Constitution, the largest paper in Georgia, and The Wichita Eagle, the largest paper in Kansas, illustrate the significant withdrawal by regional papers from distant counties.

The Constitution was one of the first Southern papers to support the Civil Rights movement. The newsrooms of the Journal-Constitution (which operated separately until 2001) attracted esteemed editors throughout the 20th century, and their journalism has been recognized through the years with numerous awards, including Pulitzer Prizes for Public Service, Editorial Writing and Investigative Reporting. As such, the Journal-Constitution exercised influence that stretched beyond its borders, and it often set the agenda for debate of topics important to the South.

Georgia has 159 counties – more than any other state except Texas, which is much larger geographically. At its peak in the late 1980s and early 1990s, the Journal-Constitution papers combined circulated in all 159 counties, plus some adjacent counties in South Carolina and Florida. In 1996, the Journal-Constitution had a paid circulation of 426,000 and was still available in 124 counties. By 2004, the Journal-Constitution's circulation had dipped to 386,000, and was available in 89 of the state's 159 counties. In 2019, it circulated only 111,000 copies in 32 counties.[53]

The Wichita Eagle has played a similar role in identifying issues that were uniquely important to that state. Additionally, the paper's editor gained national attention in the 1990s for pioneering "public journalism," which used polling and other journalistic means to involve residents in identifying important community issues and encouraging their engagement in civic affairs. In 1992, the Eagle had a paid circulation of 120,000 and was available in more than 70 of 110 counties in Kansas. By 2004, the paper still had a circulation of 90,000, but was distributed in only 24 counties. By 2019, print circulation had decreased to 41,000, and The Eagle was distributed in only 10 counties adjacent to the Wichita metro area. The paper was printed in Kansas City, Missouri, (200 miles away) in early evening, then shipped back to Wichita for distribution. The Eagle, still the largest paper in Kansas, had effectively pulled back coverage to its home market.[54]

As print circulations have declined, there's been an increased interest in attracting more digital subscriptions. However, newspapers are struggling to get online subscribers to pay the approximate amount for online access that they do for print subscriptions.

DECLINE IN ATLANTA JOURNAL CONSTITUTION DISTRIBUTION BY COUNTY: 1996-2019

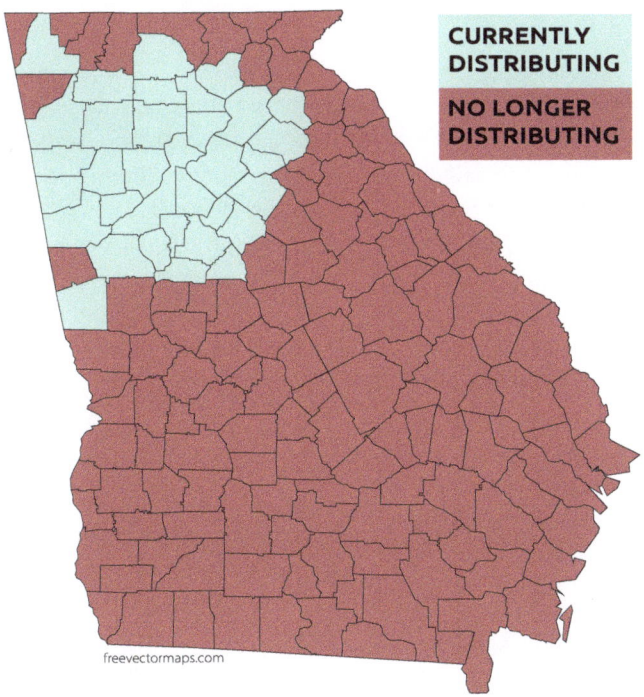

CURRENTLY DISTRIBUTING

NO LONGER DISTRIBUTING

freevectormaps.com

The Atlanta Journal Constitution circulates in just 32 counties in Georgia, compared to 124 counties in 1996.

SOURCE: Standard Rate and Data Service (SRDS)

Even the nation's largest papers, including The New York Times, charge online subscribers "introductory rates" that amount to only a fraction of what they charge for the print edition.[55]

Many metro newspapers that once had hundreds of thousands of print subscribers have been able to entice only a few thousand subscribers to pay for their online editions, at only 23 percent of the price charged print subscribers.[56] Also, research has shown that while charging for online access may boost revenue and profit in the first and second years, that uptick levels off in the third year, unless publishers think of creative ways to reach nonsubscribers, such as free e-newsletters.[57]

Although many small dailies and weeklies now also charge for online subscriptions, they have even less opportunity to increase the price for their print and online subscriptions than the

regional papers. This is especially true for small papers located in poorer communities. As a result, many still charge approximately the same amount for their print editions as they did a decade ago – and are even more constrained in what they can charge for online subscriptions.

While today print and online subscriptions may account for a much higher percentage of overall revenue than in 2004 at both large dailies and small community papers – as much as 50 percent compared with 15 percent in 2004 – the increased circulation share is due to the counterbalancing decrease in print advertising revenue. In other words, publishers are replacing the loss of high-margin print advertising revenue with low-margin subscription revenue, further depressing their already slim profit margins.

WHERE HAVE ALL THE JOURNALISTS GONE?

Newspapers have historically employed many more reporters than any other news organizations and, as a consequence, have produced the majority of the news that feeds our democracy.[58] Over the past decade, the number of newspaper journalists fell by half from 71,000 to 35,000.[59] Even though the number of journalists employed at digital sites doubled to 16,000 and those at television stations rose slightly to 30,000, there was an overall loss of more than 24,000 journalists in the field, which translates into thousands of stories that did not get covered – at both the local and regional level. Researchers at Duke University found that during a seven-day period in 2016, there was not a single locally produced news story in any news outlet in 20 of the 100 mid-sized communities they surveyed.[60]

The loss of journalists always results in a loss of journalism, as editors have to make hard decisions about which stories to cover and which to ignore. Both transparency and accountability suffer. Approximately two-thirds of the newspaper journalists who have vanished were employed on the large dailies, and the rest were employed by weeklies or small dailies that closed or merged. When a small weekly or daily closes, there is no reporter to cover routine government meetings or breaking news. When a regional daily newspaper lays off veteran journalists, the major investigative pieces that expose corruption and wrongdoing are not written.

In a May 2020 column, the Poynter Institute's media critic, Tom Jones, asked, "Why did it take so long for the Ahmaud Arbery shooting in Brunswick, Georgia, to become one of the biggest stories in the country?" A reporter for the local paper, The Brunswick News, first reported on the shooting of Arbery, a black man shot by two white men while jogging, in late February 2020 when it occurred. But the story only attracted state and national attention two months later when it was reported by The Atlanta Journal-Constitution and The New York Times. Brunswick, Jones points out, is an hour from Jacksonville, Florida, but covered by neither the regional television station nor the Jacksonville newspaper, and the local newspaper in Brunswick has only four journalists on staff. He goes on to note: "A big reason it took so long for this story to

become a major one: where it happened. Brunswick, Georgia, isn't quite in a news desert, but it's close. … The biggest paper in Georgia – and a well-respected news outlet – is the Atlanta Journal-Constitution. But Atlanta is more than 300 miles away from Brunswick and the AJC does not have a bureau there. The only time the AJC covers that area of the state is for breaking bad weather, such as a hurricane, or climate coverage."[61]

In the latter half of the 20th century, when circulation and newsroom staffing were at their highest levels, major metro and regional papers employed hundreds in their newsrooms. This included not only investigative reporters, but also beat reporters covering education, health and politics, as well as regional reporters who roamed the state and often identified local problems that were about to become state and national concerns. Ambitious journalism won accolades and prizes for the large state and metro newspapers in the 20th century, but it came with a steep price tag for the newspaper. As print advertising collapsed, the largest dailies began downsizing their reporting staffs. In the mid 1990s – when The News and Observer of Raleigh won the Pulitzer Public Service Award for its investigative series on the environmental issues posed by large-scale industrial hog farming in eastern North Carolina – the paper had more than 250 journalists in its newsroom and fanned out across the state. At the end of 2019, it had only 60 journalists.[62]

Staffing has been so dramatically pared at many state and metro dailies that the remaining journalists complain they cannot adequately cover their cities, to say nothing of the outlying regions. Multiple rounds of layoffs have decimated some of the largest metro papers. At the Denver Post, layoffs over a five-year period reduced the number of journalists from 180 in 2013 – when the paper received a Pulitzer Prize for coverage of a mass shooting at a cinema in Aurora – to fewer than 70 journalists in 2018, responsible for covering a metro area with 2 million residents.[63] Layoffs at the New York Daily News in 2018 left only 50 reporters to cover the city's 8 million residents. More recently, in April and May 2020, The [Cleveland] Plain Dealer, which had more than 350 employed in its newsroom in the early 2000s, laid

DECLINE OF TOTAL U.S. NEWSROOM EMPLOYMENT: 2004-2019

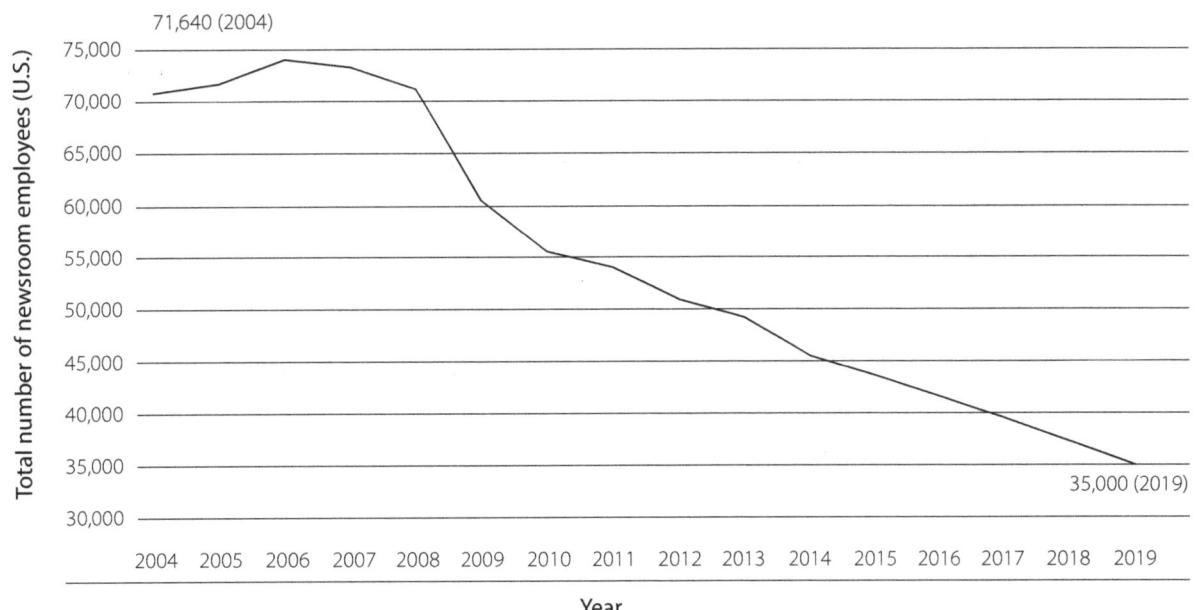

Overall newsroom employment has declined 50 percent since 2004.

off the remaining 30 journalists on the unionized print newspaper, leaving approximately 60 nonunionized journalists employed by Cleveland.com responsible for covering northeastern Ohio, an area with more than 4 million people.[64]

The coverage provided by journalists at the large metro and regional papers has had immense economic benefit for society as a whole.[65] Over his career, the senior investigative reporter on the News & Observer's Pulitzer-Prize-winning series on hog farms pursued 150 investigations – on everything from water quality to highway safety – that led to the passage and adoption of dozens of state laws and regulations.[66]

There is also evidence that journalistic competition between regional dailies and smaller community papers also spurs more thorough coverage of the issues by reporters on the smaller papers, who lack the resources that the larger papers can bring to bear.[67] Larry Hobbs, the reporter on The Brunswick News who covered the Arbery shooting, told Poynter's media critic that The Times story made "a huge difference," because "it was thorough, and really well done, as you would expect from The New York Times ... And I'm glad they did it. It put a big spotlight on this story and this story needed that spotlight."[68]

As the number of journalists has declined in recent years, interest in job security has increased among those still employed. The national organization, NewsGuild/ Communication Workers of America, grew by nearly 3,000 new members from 2018 to 2020. Unions were recognized at large metro papers, such as The Los Angeles Times, with 359 members, and The Miami Herald, with 99, and smaller regional ones, such as The Roanoke Times in Virginia, with 51 members, and the South Bend Tribune in Indiana, with 29.[69]

However, the loss of thousands of veteran journalists has already taken a toll on the quality and quality of journalism that is being produced today at the large regional dailies. When beat and investigative reporters at metro newspapers retire or are laid off, they often are replaced by less-experienced reporters who lack the training and skills to produce major journalistic pieces. In the 1990s, the country's five largest newspapers (in terms of circulation and journalists) received less than a third of the most prestigious investigative journalism awards, with the rest being awarded to journalists on the country's regional dailies. By 2013, the country's largest newspapers were consistently receiving more than half of those annual awards.[70]

Also, many of the editors at metro papers who oversaw major projects, and mentored less experienced journalists, have been laid off. "This raises questions of when and where the next generation of journalists focused on accountability work will get trained, particularly those who might focus on local institutions," according to Stanford economist James T. Hamilton.[71]

THE FUTURE OF NEWSPAPERS

With readers and journalists vanishing – along with print advertising – can newspapers survive? In 2004, most industry observers assumed that digital revenue would replace lost print revenue and that most of the successful newspapers of 2020 would be well on the way to digital-only content and delivery. But that transition has proved very difficult, with the two tech giants – Facebook and Google – capturing a majority of digital dollars. This leaves legacy newspapers competing with other media – television, radio, magazines and online startups – for the digital leftovers. Complicating matters, digital pricing of both advertising and subscriptions favors very large organizations, such as the tech giants that reach hundreds of millions. As a result, newspapers are caught between two worlds – continuing to incur most of the costs associated with the print world and reaping very little of the anticipated digital revenue.

National papers, such as The New York Times and Wall Street Journal, have focused on attracting a sizable online audience, willing and able to pay a premium to get the unique news and information they offer, in the hopes they can then attract advertisers willing to pay a premium to reach these affluent and engaged online audiences. In 2019, The New York Times added a million digital-only subscribers and had more than 5.3 million subscribers to all its print and digital products, including the Crossword and Cooking publications. Total subscription revenue of $1 billion was twice the advertising revenue. Even so, slightly more than half of the newspaper's total advertising and subscription revenue still came from the print edition of the paper. Digital advertising revenue in 2019 had actually decreased by more than 6 percent compared with the previous year – not a promising sign.[72] That The Times still depends on the print edition for half of its revenue illustrates how difficult it can be for legacy papers to make the digital transformation.

Since most metro and state dailies have already pared distribution to outlying areas and cut newsroom staffing

THE RAPID DECLINE OF LEGACY MEDIA AND THE METEORIC RISE OF DIGITAL
Distribution of digital vs. newspaper advertising spending in the US from 2010 to 2020

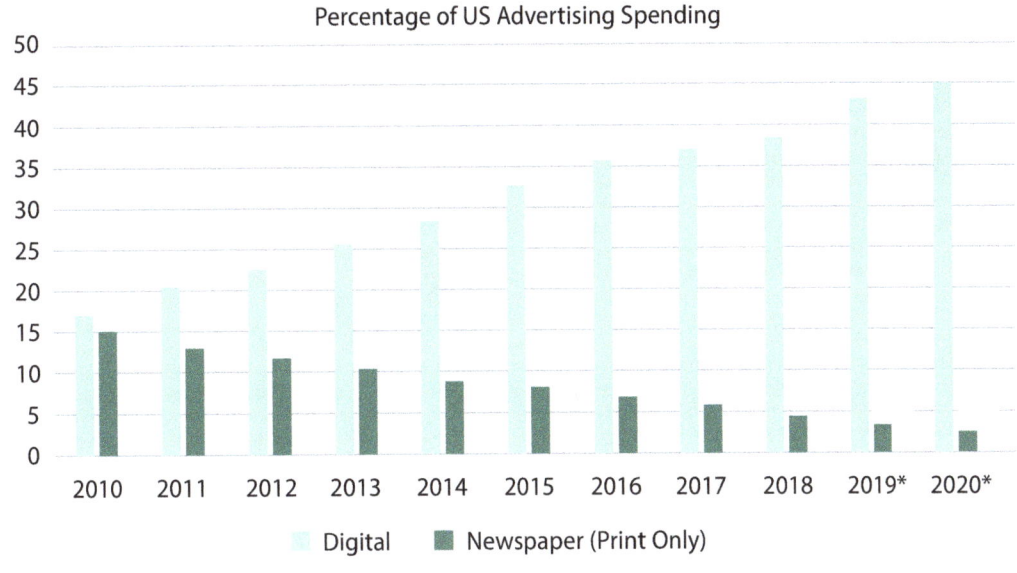

Percentage of US Advertising Spending

Source: eMarketer, Statista 2020

to skeletal levels, their owners have only one other place to seek significant cost savings – converting print subscribers to digital delivery and cutting back on daily publication of a print edition. Even at their peak in the latter part of the 20th century – in terms of revenue and circulation – most daily papers were only profitable three days a week. Those were the three heavy advertising days: Sunday with its display and classified advertising, as well as the slick inserts offering coupons from national retailers and manufacturers; Wednesday or Thursday, with the local grocery advertisements; and Friday, with the weekend advertisements for movies, events and other entertainment. Sunday was especially profitable, accounting for more than half of total advertising revenue. These three days financed the distribution of the paper seven days a week.

Ironically, even though a majority of readers have preferred to get their news online since 2011, the subscribers to print editions have been very reluctant to give up their habit of reading a physical copy. Although many large dailies have focused in recent years on increasing the number of digital subscribers, research for an international newspaper association found that those efforts to date have been largely disappointing, resulting in only a few thousand subscribers to e-editions at most major metros. So publishers of major metros have proceeded gingerly, decreasing print publication and distribution days gradually, one day at a time. In 2019, for example, McClatchy announced it would decrease publication of all its papers from seven days to six.[73]

Suddenly discontinuing daily publication can backfire, especially for large dailies, with loyal, but aging, readers. In 2013, Advance Publications announced it was taking a number of its daily newspapers, including the Times-Picayune in New Orleans, from seven days to three days.[74] That precipitated an uproar from readers and a competitive response from a paper in Baton Rouge, which started publishing and distributing an edition in New

Orleans. A year after announcing the cutback, Advance Publications reversed course and began printing a tabloid-sized paper in New Orleans the other four days of the week, but it was too late to recoup the goodwill of readers and advertisers. In 2019, The Advocate of Baton Rouge purchased The Times-Picayune and nola.com, laying off 161 employees, including 65 journalists.[75]

The publisher of the Arkansas Democrat-Gazette, a family-owned and -operated newspaper in Little Rock, opted for a more aggressive approach in 2019 – converting to digital delivery Monday through Saturday, with a Sunday-only print publication, distributed throughout the state. But he did so only after doing extensive reader research and analysis. Over the course of one and a half years, the paper spent $13 million purchasing iPads for its current print subscribers and sent as many as 70 "trainers" across the state to teach readers how to use the technology to have a better online experience with the newspaper. Executives calculated that the key to profitability was converting at least 70 percent of current print subscribers to iPad delivery at the same amount – $37 a month – as they pay to read the print editions. At the end of 2019, the paper reported conversion rates that exceeded 80 percent, and were as high as 100 percent. Since the Sunday paper was still attracting significant advertising and was profitable, the paper opted to continue printing and distributing a Sunday paper for the time being.[76]

With the economic fallout from the coronavirus pandemic resulting in dramatic declines in advertising, other dailies are making similar moves in 2020, but without the underlying research conducted by the Democrat-Gazette. Citing a major drop in advertising, The Tampa Bay Times was one of the first large papers to announce it was "temporarily" cutting back print publication to Sunday and Wednesday only, and would publish e-editions the other five days.[77] Industry analysts doubt those papers that cut back in 2020 will resume daily print publication once the virus is under control. At that point, the real test for the large dailies will be whether readers renew their subscriptions and are finally willing to pay as much to read the paper online as they did to read the print version.

While successfully converting to digital-only delivery may offer a lifeline to the large regional and metro papers – especially if they can get their tens of thousands of subscribers to pay for the e-edition – small dailies and weeklies cannot rely on digital subscriber or advertising revenue to contribute significantly to the bottom line. For one thing, many of these papers have only a few thousand print subscribers – and very limited ability to increase the price of a subscription, especially those in economically struggling communities. Most small dailies and weeklies are further constrained by the small size of their markets and the number and size of local businesses that want to advertise.

Although small weeklies and dailies – especially those located in communities that are growing in population and are relatively affluent – can have higher profit margins than large dailies, they generate much less cash. A great proportion of their costs are fixed, so they have much less flexibility in terms of cutting expenses. Therefore, in order to succeed, publishers of weeklies and small dailies have to focus the majority of their attention on bringing

in new sources of revenue – nondigital, as well as digital, from advertisers, as well as subscribers. One publisher of a small weekly described such a strategy as "breaking out of jail" – looking beyond the geographic boundaries of the community where the newspaper is located to other markets and other opportunities to grow revenue.[78] This can involve publishing glossy lifestyle magazines as well as staid phone directories, sponsoring in-person events, producing podcasts and videos, and establishing in-house digital agencies and e-commerce sites to serve local merchants. The key is diversifying, mixing and matching digital and nondigital products and services for both advertisers and readers, in an attempt to replace the lost print advertising revenue they historically relied on.

But, as the coronavirus has demonstrated, many forces are beyond the control of individual publishers of newspapers. With profit margins at most newspapers in the single digits, a bad quarter can sink both small weeklies, as well as large dailies. In 2020, many newspapers are looking at back-to-back money-losing quarters. The stakes – for both large dailies and small weeklies – have never been higher. Successfully transitioning readers to digital delivery may well save many dailies. The small weeklies and dailies, however, will need to continue to be both creative and disciplined in their strategies.

THE NEW MEDIA GIANTS

Key Takeaways

(1) The large hedge funds and private equity groups that purchased distressed newspaper chains in recent years introduced a new management philosophy that focused on bottom-line performance to the exclusion of journalism's civic mission. As revenues and profit margins fell sharply, these practices were widely adopted by other newspaper companies, leading to major cost-cutting initiatives and almost no investment in innovation.

(2) Despite the shrinking universe of surviving papers, the chains are bigger than ever – and, at the beginning of 2020, they were poised to grow even bigger, with the creation of highly leveraged mega-chains formed by the union of large publicly traded newspaper companies with large hedge funds and private equity chains. Privately held regional chains are also growing rapidly.

(3) Massive consolidation in the newspaper industry has shifted editorial and business decisions to a few large corporations without strong ties to the communities where their papers are located. This raises questions about the future journalistic and business viability of the very largest chains.

In 2017, Japan's telecommunications conglomerate Softbank Group purchased the investment firm Fortress Investment Group, which managed more than $70 billion in various assets, including real estate firms, private railways, golf courses and debt collection agencies.[79] Though it went largely unreported at the time, Fortress also owned and managed the country's largest newspaper chain, Gatehouse, which, at the time, operated more than 400 newspapers in 36 states. By the end of 2019, the Gatehouse chain had ballooned to more than 600 papers, by purchasing the country's second-largest newspaper company, Gannett. Gatehouse immediately shed its old name and began operating as the "new" Gannett, having adopted the name of the century-old newspaper enterprise it had acquired.[80]

The purchase of a U.S. newspaper chain by a Japanese company is emblematic of the dramatic and dizzying change in the industry in recent years. New ownership structures, backed by complex – and often opaque – financial transactions, have transformed family-centered media businesses into diversified, highly leveraged investment entities that prioritize shareholder return over producing all the news that's fit to print or publish online.

The media barons of the 21st century – hedge funds, private equity firms and other investment entities – swept onto the scene in the years immediately following the 2008 recession when they began aggressively purchasing hundreds of distressed newspapers and chains, many in bankruptcy proceedings. Their rise displaced the media barons of the 20th century – the large publicly traded and privately held chains – such as Gannett, Knight Ridder, Hearst and Advance. They employed the same disruptive business models they used in other industries – many of them adopted by the surviving chains as the fortunes of the newspaper industry continued to decline. They financed their acquisitions with significant debt and managed their highly leveraged newspapers through aggressive cost-cutting and revenue goals, paired with financial and pension restructuring, including bankruptcy. To reduce costs, they laid off staff, froze wages, reduced benefits and consolidated sales and editorial functions in regional hubs, far removed from the community where the paper was located. Profits derived from cost cutting were not reinvested; instead, they were used to pay loans, management fees and shareholder dividends.

LARGEST 10 OWNERS IN 2019 RANKED BY NUMBER OF PAPERS OWNED

OWNER TYPE: PUBLIC/ INVESTMENT   INVESTMENT   PRIVATE

Rank	Owner Name	Total Papers	Daily Papers	Total Circ. 000s
1	Gannett/Gatehouse	613	262	8,596
2	Digital First/Tribune	207	70	5,163
3	Lee/BH Media	170	84	2,464
4	Adams Publishing Group	158	40	1,233
5	CNHI	112	71	993
6	Ogden Newspapers	84	49	851
7	Paxton Media Group	75	42	575
8	Boone Newspapers	65	29	458
9	Community Media Group	57	14	331
10	Landmark Media Enterprises	55	3	443

At their peak in 2016, six of the 10 largest newspaper chains were owned and operated by private equity firms or other investment entities. These six firms owned 15 percent of all papers in the country. In recent years, as print revenue has continued to decline, and efforts to significantly increase digital advertising revenue have failed, some of the smallest firms – such as Civitas and 10/13 – headed for the exit. Others, such as Community Newspaper Holdings, Inc., owned by the state pension fund of Alabama, have been unable to sell their chains, and have, instead, downsized by closing and merging unprofitable weeklies, including 12 in April and May 2020.

However, the largest chains, including Gatehouse and Digital First, have decided, at least for the moment, to double down and acquire or merge with other large chains – specifically the last remaining publicly traded firms – in hopes of gaining "synergies" on the cost side and shoring up sagging revenue trends.

In late 2019, Gatehouse took on $1.8 billion in debt, financed at 11.5 percent interest by another private equity firm, Apollo Global Management, to purchase Gannett.[81] BH Media, owned by Berkshire Hathaway, asked Lee Enterprises to assume day-to-day management of its 79 papers in 2018, and then in early 2020, Berkshire Hathaway sold the chain to Lee. Berkshire Hathaway also provided $576 million in long-term financing at 9 percent interest to cover both the acquisition and refinancing of $400 million in debt Lee still carried on the books from earlier acquisitions.[82] Rebuffed in its effort to merge with Gannett, Alden Capital, which owns and operates the Digital First chain, amassed more than a third of outstanding shares of the Tribune's stock in an attempt to force a merger.[83] Alden Capital has also taken a minority stake in Lee Enterprises. McClatchy, the last of the remaining publicly traded chains, filed for bankruptcy protection in February 2020. It will emerge from bankruptcy owned by the hedge fund Chatham Asset Management, which has considering auctioning off the entire chain. One likely option is that McClatchy will merge with Tribune.

These hybrid chains – a merger of a private equity firm and a traditional publicly traded chain with shares that can be bought and traded on the New York Stock Exchange – appear to be poised to exert tremendous influence on the future of the newspaper industry. They control the fate of more than 1,000 papers, including a third of the nation's dailies, and more than half of total daily circulation.

However, their ride at the top may be fleeting. By the end of April 2020, Gannett, Lee and Tribune had all announced furloughs and pay cuts to compensate for the significant drop in revenue their papers experienced as the economy shut down abruptly to deal with coronavirus.[84] There were indications that additional layoffs would follow, as all of them were lobbying for federal funds to shore up their rapidly declining bottom lines. Lee Enterprises stock had fallen from $2 a share at the beginning of 2020 to less than a dollar, and Tribune was trading at $8 a share, down from $13. Gannett, which had also suspended the dividend on its shares, had taken the biggest tumble, from $6 a share at the time of the merger in late 2019 to about $1 at the end of April.[85]

While it is too early to know whether these hybrid mega-chains will survive for long, the business practices introduced by these relative newcomers – the financiers – as well as the exponential growth of chains in recent years, pose new and difficult societal and economic issues.

THE GOLIATHS GROW BIGGER

Even as the universe of newspapers shrinks, newspaper chains are bigger than ever – and are poised to potentially grow even bigger in the months ahead. Over the past 15 years, the number of newspaper owners decreased by more than a third, from about 4,000 to 2,400, with large chains gobbling up smaller regional chains, as well as locally owned dailies and weeklies. More than a dozen of the largest chains in 2004 – including Knight Ridder, Media General, Pulitzer, Journal Register and Media News – no longer exist. At the same time, companies that did not exist 15 years ago have acquired dozens of papers in recent years and now are among the biggest owners.

The fate of more and more newspapers is in the hands of the largest 25 or so chains. At the end of 2004, the largest 25 chains (as measured by number of papers, not circulation) owned only a fifth of the 8,900 papers and less than a third of the 1,472 dailies. Fifteen years later, the 25 largest chains own a third of the 6,700 surviving newspapers in the country and 70 percent of the 1,260 dailies. While the biggest 25 chains own 2,156 papers, including 863 dailies, the next largest group – 26 through 50 – owns only 445 newspapers and 54 dailies.

As chains have grown in size, the ownership structure of the newspaper industry has changed dramatically. In the latter years of the 20th century the large publicly traded firms – including Gannett, Knight Ridder, Lee Enterprises and Pulitzer – supplanted the large privately held chains, using the money they raised by issuing stock to become aggressive buyers of other newspapers. In the wake of the 2008 recession, the publicly traded firms were supplanted by the private equity and hedge owners, who purchased hundreds of papers in bankruptcy proceedings for bargain prices – two to five times annual earnings compared with 13 times earnings in 2007.[86] Chains became bigger than ever. In 2004, the largest chain, Gannett, which was publicly traded, owned 177 papers. A decade later, the largest chain was the private-equity financed Gatehouse group, with 379 papers.

At the start of the third decade of the 21st century, the ownership structure is morphing yet again as the largest private equity and hedge fund newspaper owners merge with the last of the surviving publicly traded companies. The very biggest chains dwarf the others. In 2020, the largest chains – Gannett/Gatehouse, Tribune/Digital First, and Lee/BH Media – own 15 percent of all newspapers (990) and a third (416) of all dailies, including some of the largest in the country, and control more than half of all circulation. By comparison, the next seven largest chains – 4 through 10 – own a total of only 600 newspapers and only 258 dailies.

However, another ownership trend has also been emerging. As newspaper revenue has continued to decline, so have valuations of newspapers, which are at historic lows. As the economy began to recover from the recession in 2013 and 2014, some of the smaller privately owned national and regional chains, which were largely debt-free, began quietly and selectively purchasing papers. As the private equity companies – such as Civitas and 10/13 – sold their papers, these private chains – such as Hearst and Adams – bought those papers, as well as smaller family-owned properties, such as the fourth-generation Jones Media, headquartered in Tennessee.[87]

The most active purchasers in the years leading up to 2020 include century-old national private chains, such as Hearst, as well as smaller chains, such as Ogden, Boone and Paxton. Boone, a chain based in Alabama, almost doubled in size between 2004 and 2019, growing from 37 newspapers to 65. New companies were also formed, including AIM in 2012 and Adams Publishing in 2013, both established by CEOs with extensive newspaper and financial experience.[88] In 2014, Adams owned only 38 newspapers. By 2020, it was the fourth-largest chain in the country with 158 newspapers spread across the upper South and Midwest. AIM, the 13th-largest chain in the country, owns 46, mostly in Texas, Indiana and Ohio.

LARGEST 25 OWNERS IN 2020 RANKED BY NUMBER OF PAPERS OWNED

OWNER TYPE: PUBLIC/ INVESTMENT   INVESTMENT   PRIVATE

Rank	Owner Name	Total Papers	Daily Papers	Total Circ. (000s)
1	Gannett/Gatehouse	613	262	8,596
2	Digital First/Tribune	207	70	5,163
3	Lee/BH Media	170	84	2,464
4	Adams Publishing Group	158	40	1,233
5	CNHI	112	71	993
6	Ogden Newspapers	84	49	851
7	Paxton Media Group	75	42	575
8	Boone Newspapers	65	29	458
9	Community Media Group	57	14	331
10	Landmark Media Enterprises	55	3	443
11	Hearst Corporation	51	22	1,296
12	McClatchy	47	30	1,747
13	Aim Media	46	26	405
14	News Media Corporation	43	3	183
15	Black Press Group	42	10	777
16	Rust Communications	41	17	239
17	Advance Publications	41	16	1,545
18	Shaw Media	39	10	269
19	Horizon Publications	37	23	162
20	Forum Communications	35	10	276
21	Morris Multimedia	30	3	205
22	Trib Publications	29		91
23	Sample Media Group	27	16	163
24	Wick Communications	26	10	154
25	Community Newspapers Inc. (CNI)	26	3	170

By the end of 2019, 20 of the largest 25 newspaper chains, as measured by number of newspapers owned, were privately held companies. In total they owned almost 1,000 papers. They ranged in size from Community Newspapers Inc., the 25th largest with 26 newspapers in Georgia and the Carolinas, to Adams. While all but Adams are less than half the size of the hybrid mega-chains, they were growing rapidly in the years leading up to 2020. These chains consist of several dozen papers – mostly weeklies – in small and mid-sized communities, not the highly competitive metro markets favored by the mega-chains. Most keep a low profile and are unknown outside the regions where they are headquartered.

The 21st century regional chains have more in common with the private chains that dominated in the early half of 20th century than the publicly traded and financed newspaper companies of today. Often a family member is at the head of the company – for example, David Paxton is CEO of the Paducah, Kentucky, media group that bears his family's name. Some, such as Adams, are known for retaining family members as publishers and editors when they purchase a newspaper, others for bringing in new management. Some, such as Morris Multimedia, encourage innovative journalistic and business approaches, and own a variety of media properties, including television stations and digital properties. All operate their newspapers as small businesses, with a singular focus on the bottom line and cash flow. In contrast to the mega-chains, they have lean corporate staffs and tend to keep low levels of debt. So, when hard times hit, they do not have to worry about paying off loans on "underwater" properties. As a result, they tend to buy and hold properties, instead of trading them.[89]

Going into the 2020 recession, there were two very different ownership models among the largest chains: the high-profile, highly leveraged mega-chain versus the low-profile, low-debt smaller regional chain. Industry analysts are predicting that a prolonged and deep recession resulting from the coronavirus could lead to the closure of hundreds of newspapers and, potentially, the bankruptcy of the chains that are highly leveraged. If so, 2020 could represent the high-water mark of the large hybrid mega-chains, and perhaps pave the way for a new type of ownership structure dominated by the rapidly ascending privately held regional chains.

NEW URGENCY FOR AN AGE-OLD DEBATE

As the 20th-century business model for newspapers collapses, it brings to the forefront issues around obligations to shareholders versus journalism's civic mission.[90] Massive consolidation in the newspaper industry – coupled with the recent widespread adoption of the business practices and philosophies of private equity and hedge funds – has shifted editorial and business decisions to owners and corporations without a strong stake in the local communities where their papers are located. As chains have grown bigger and bigger, it has become harder and harder to discern the financial and journalism priorities of local newspapers or to hold them accountable.

The debate is an old one, but with a new sense of urgency. A recent survey by Gallup found that while trust in local news organizations was higher than for large national news outlets, it is declining rapidly.[91] Numerous rounds of layoffs at the large chains of today have left skeletal newsrooms with beleaguered editors and reporters struggling to provide timely and comprehensive news coverage of their communities. Almost half of the 35,000 people the Pew Research Center surveyed in 2018 noted a decrease in the quantity and quality of news they were receiving from their local newspapers, but three-quarters were unaware of the financial difficulties their local newspapers were facing.[92]

When Scripps and Hearst assembled the first large privately owned chains in the 1920s, concerns were immediately voiced about the span of influence they could wield across multiple markets. These concerns faded as radio and television amassed even greater audiences. Many scholars, policymakers and journalists voiced new concerns about the civic responsibility of chains in the 1980s and 1990s, as some of the largest chains – including Gannett, Knight Ridder, McClatchy and Pulitzer – issued stock and began managing the expectations of Wall Street investors and analysts.[93]

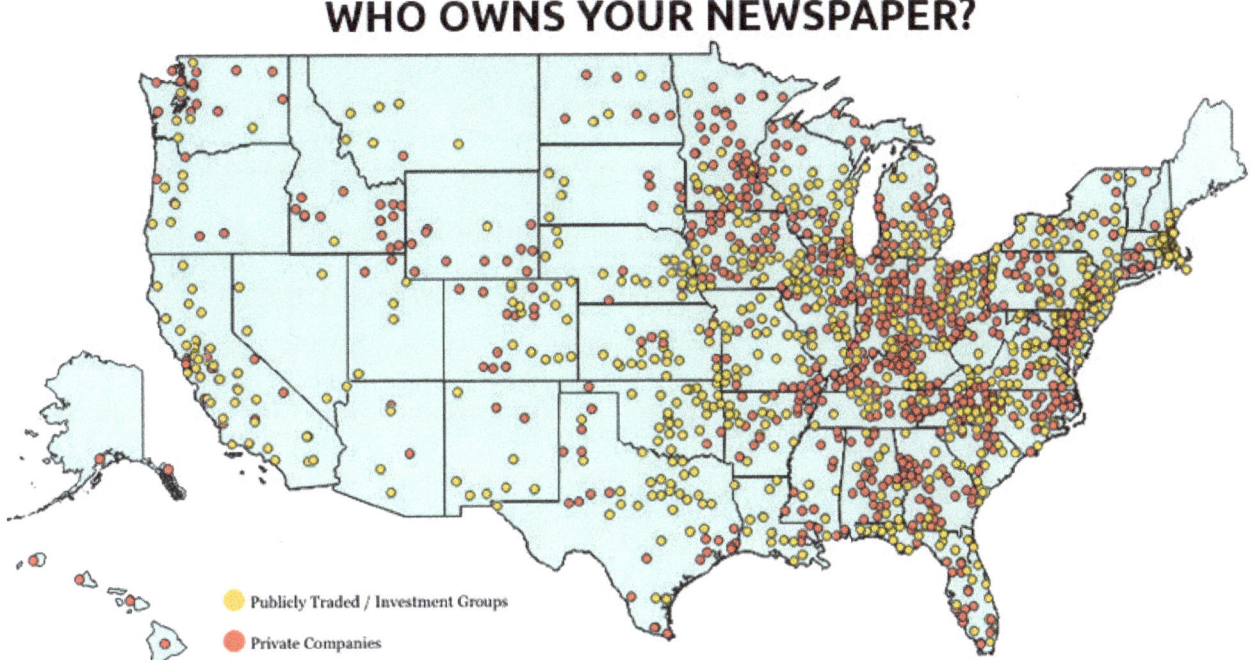

WHO OWNS YOUR NEWSPAPER?

● Publicly Traded / Investment Groups
● Private Companies

The largest 25 newspaper chains own a third of all newspapers in the U.S., up from one-fifth in 2004.

Source: UNC Hussman School of Journalism and Media

However, there was a financial incentive for even the most bottom-line-focused publicly traded companies to balance profits with civic duty. Since most newspapers in the latter half of the 20th century sold for at least 13 times annual earnings, chains had a financial incentive to "buy and hold" the newspapers they purchased. This encouraged the publicly traded chains to establish roots in the communities where their newspapers were located. They built new plants, purchased state-of-the-art presses and expanded circulation and distribution to outlying regions. The most civic-minded of the publicly traded chains invested in their journalism by establishing bureaus in Washington, D.C., and other major cities, including international capitals, and forming news services, similar to the Associated Press, to share the news articles produced by journalists in these bureaus with other papers in the company.

There was also a level of financial transparency, since publicly traded companies are required to submit quarterly and annual reports with audited financial statements and management assessments to the Securities and Exchange Commission. This allowed shareholders – as well as policymakers, scholars and community activists – to scrutinize and judge both the journalistic and business accomplishments of these large publicly traded companies.

The takeover of newspaper chains in the early 21st century by private investment entities with complex and convoluted ownership patterns and financial transactions has posed a new and urgent set of concerns around transparency, accountability and civic mission. In contrast to publicly traded newspaper companies, the closely held hedge funds and private equity firms that own newspapers are required to disclose only the most basic information in their annual shareholder statements. So, there is almost no transparency, making it difficult to decipher the financial decisions made by the company, identify the largest shareholders or learn the compensation of the funds' executives and managers.

There is also no transparency around their journalistic decisions. Their stated mission is to earn money for their shareholders, and comments from executives suggest they prioritize profitability over any civic mission.[94] Judging by their actions, instead of investing in their newly acquired papers, these chains focus on cutting costs to prop up profits and then using those profits to pay management fees, interest on loans or shareholder dividends. Newspapers often represent only a small portion of their portfolio of companies that can span the globe. Alden Capital, for example, has used profits from its Digital First newspaper chain to prop up failed investments in a Canadian pharmacy chain and Greek debt.[95]

In contrast to the traditional publicly traded and private chains of the 20th century, the investment-owned chains do not buy and hold properties. They view newspapers as short-term investments, and they hold newspapers to the same financial benchmarks as manufacturing plants or health care facilities. They actively manage their holdings, selling or closing underperforming properties. In recent years, there has been a constant reshuffling of the deck, with more than half of all surviving newspapers changing hands over the past decade, many sold two or more times by the large investment entities.

This constant turnover in ownership and trading of newspapers significantly weakens bonds between news organizations and the communities where they are located. Editors and publishers often cycle in and out of a community in a matter of months, never putting down roots. Another round of layoffs occurs with every transaction, leaving skeletal staffs on many newspapers. Sales, editing and back-shop functions are outsourced to remote locations, with regional editors and publishers responsible for multiple newspapers. Over time, this leads to the merger of two or more smaller papers into one paper – and the closure of the smaller paper. Most of the communities that have lost papers in recent years have above-average poverty rates and below-average household incomes. Once the hometown paper closes, residents in those markets are left without a reliable source of local information. This has led to the simultaneous rise of news deserts – communities without a local news outlet – and "ghost newspapers," with depleted newsrooms that are only a shadow of their former selves.

The newspapers chains of the 20th century provided economic benefits for shareholders and, arguably, societal benefits. Larger chains were in a better position to negotiate on price with vendors, including paper manufacturers, and offer national and regional advertisers access to multiple markets. By owning newspapers in multiple cities, chains could also pool journalistic resources and provide newspaper subscribers in even the smallest communities with a varied menu of state and national news, as well as local news.

But chain ownership in the 21st century offers many fewer economic and societal benefits, especially for the large newspaper companies. The collapse of the for-profit business model for print newspapers has sent projections on advertising revenue plummeting year to year, which means recent mergers and acquisitions are most often justified as "cost-saving measures." When Gatehouse announced it was purchasing Gannett, the company foresaw no revenue growth for the foreseeable future, but cost savings of almost $300 million.[96] Invariably, such promises for savings result in several rounds of layoffs of journalists, which, in turn, mean a loss of local news and a diminishment of societal benefits. Plus, many of these large mergers and acquisition are highly leveraged, which places a premium on extracting even more earnings from operations to pay down the debt.

As the era of the print newspaper recedes into history, the economic rationale for the large chains of today abates.[97] In the print era, there was a premium on operational excellence at each newspaper in a chain. The business operations at each paper were largely independent of those at another. In the digital age, there is a premium on organizational flexibility, fluid

NUMBER OF ANNUAL NEWSPAPER TRANSACTIONS 2007-2019

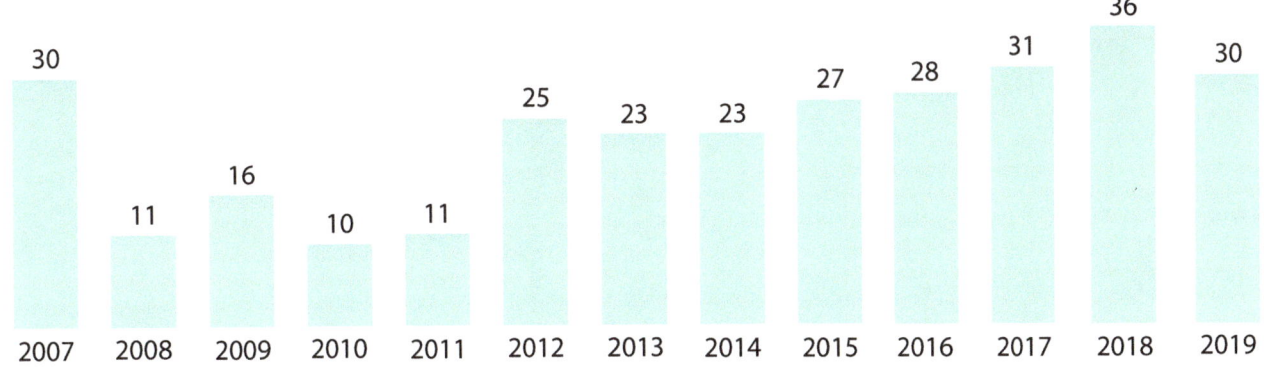

Transactions involving daily newspapers peaked in 2018.

SOURCE: Dirks, Van Essen, Murray & April

partnerships and engagement of audiences around special interests, including geographic concerns. This calls into question the long-term economic viability of large national chains in the 21st century.[98]

The price of buying a newspaper continues to fall – from three to five times earnings in the years following the 2008 recession to less than two times earnings at the beginning of 2020. Many newspaper owners who want to sell often cannot find buyers. This drop in the cost of owning a paper could potentially open the doors to new models in the years ahead – including a rebirth of local ownership or a return to the smaller, regional chains of the early and mid-20th century.

Steven Waldman, CEO of Report for America, a national service program that places journalists in newsrooms to report on under-covered issues, suggests that the government encourage the dissolution of the large financier-backed chains by placing a moratorium on large mergers. In addition, he suggests offering a variety of tax incentives for both the large chains – encouraging them to donate or sell newspapers to local residents in a community – and consumers, allowing them to deduct the cost of a subscription.[99]

Trust in democracy's institutions begins at the grassroots level, and newspapers have historically played an important role providing the information that builds trust. But as profitability has superseded journalism's civic mission on many newspapers, the ties have become frayed and threadbare. Reviving local newspapers in the 21st century – in whatever form they take – involves not only inventing new business models, but also re-establishing journalistic priorities.

ENTREPRENEURIAL STALWARTS & START-UPS

Key Takeaways

1. A variety of legacy and start-up news outlets are currently attempting to fill the local news void, including digital sites, ethnic media, public broadcasting outlets and independently owned and operated newspapers.

2. The leaders of these enterprises are experimenting with a variety of business models, including for-profit, nonprofit, publicly funded ones, as well as hybrids and cooperatives, in which the community owns the publication.

3. Many of their endeavors show promise. But there is a critical need for more funding that would encourage the expansion of these enterprises into regions that lack a local news organization.

Throughout this country's history, strong local and regional newspapers have been both community builders and problem solvers. Publishers and editors of the most vibrant newspapers have served as a steadfast conscience in their communities and regions, exposing injustices and corruption, shining a light on the follies of corporate chieftains and bureaucrats, admonishing residents and public officials for their misdeeds and foibles, while simultaneously inspiring them with their editorials to pursue a different course. On the other hand, many in recent years – especially those owned by the large, private-equity-backed chains – have been dismissed as monopolistic tollgate operators who raised rates for advertisers and subscribers to maintain outsized profits, and failed to cover the concerns of their community, thereby giving no voice to the voiceless.

The goal in the coming years is to encourage a flowering of local news organizations that, like the very best newspapers published the 20th century, helped residents in a community solve problems by identifying the important issues of the day, encouraged economic growth and development, and nurtured social and geographic identity. As the large newspaper chains have struggled to adjust to the digital age, other news organizations have been more innovative – both with their journalism and their business models.

Entrepreneurs at digital sites, independently owned and operated newspapers, and ethnic media organizations, as well as public broadcasting outlets, have sought to thwart the rise of news deserts by providing critical news and information to underserved communities, engaging audiences on a variety of old and new platforms, even as they experiment with new business models. They have recognized that, instead of one business model that works for most organizations, as was historically the case, there will be many – for-profit, nonprofit publicly funded ones, as well as hybrids and co-operatives, in which communities own their local news organization.

Regardless of which business model they pursue, all these entrepreneurs need access to significant funding to continually experiment and develop long-term sustainable business models. And therein lies the shared challenge. Between 2005 and 2018, newspaper advertising revenue, which had historically funded local news gathering, dropped from almost $50 billion annually to less than $15 billion, resulting in the elimination of thousands of newsroom positions.[100] At the same time, nonprofit and public funding has replaced only a small fraction of the loss.

To get a more accurate assessment of the country's local news needs, our 2020 report examines the current state of the country's 525 local news digital sites, 950 ethnic media organizations, 1,400 public broadcasting outlets and 2,400 independently owned and operated newspapers.

Everyone in this country has a political, social and economic stake in whatever replaces the 20th century print version of the local newspaper, in whatever form – print, broadcast or digital. The entrepreneurial news organizations profiled in this section face significant obstacles as they attempt to fill the local news void. Nevertheless, their experiences are beginning to provide a roadmap as to how to reverse the loss of news and reach those who live in news deserts.

THE FOR-PROFIT MODEL:
Enterprising and Independent

Thanks to the establishment in recent years of hundreds of local digital news sites and ethnic media outlets, the number of independent owners and operators of for-profit local news organizations is growing in this country. All this raises the possibility of a resurgence of locally owned news outlets. Among them: The hundred-year-old Bulletin in Bend, Oregon, purchased in 2019 in a bankruptcy auction by a state-based media company, with assistance from community leaders, who helped raised the necessary funds. The Mundo Hispanico in Atlanta, purchased in 2018 by a group of Latino investors. And the Santa Cruz Local, co-founded in 2019 by two veteran journalists who had previously worked at the local paper.

Because decisions can be made locally, without consulting layers of corporate bureaucracy, independent owners and operators have much more strategic flexibility than managers of corporate-owned newspapers and can respond much more quickly to the changing needs and expectations of residents and businesses in their community. However, like most small-business owners, they typically measure revenue in the low millions or hundreds of thousands of dollars, and often have slim profit margins. So, the founders, owners, publishers and editors have to be both creative and disciplined in their approach if they are to achieve long-term financial sustainability.

Still Publishing After All These Years

Until the 1970s, most newspapers were locally owned and operated. Even though the number of independent community-based newspaper owners has declined by a third since 2004, there are still about 2,400 surviving independently owned and operated newspapers. Roughly half are located in the country's outlying suburbs and rural areas. Many are the only consistent and comprehensive source of news for their communities, which are overlooked by reporters at regional television and newspapers, except in times of disaster.

The owners of independent newspapers usually live in the communities they cover, eat at the same restaurants, shop at the same stores and attend the same events as all other residents. They put down roots, in contrast to the publishers and editors of news organizations that are part of large chains, who are often transferred from property to property every few years.[101] As a result, the fate of these independent news operations and the communities they serve is tightly intertwined, for better or worse.

Publishers of small newspapers that managed to survive have had to be especially creative in coming up with ways to diversify their revenue. With Facebook and Google collecting a majority of the digital revenue in most markets – even small ones – many independently owned newspapers still remain tethered to the print edition, still relying on print advertising and subscription revenue to pay the bills. But they are increasingly looking for ways to evolve beyond publishing a print newspaper.[102] The most successful community newspapers have aggressively sought to diversify their revenue sources by sponsoring events, creating e-newsletters and podcasts, and establishing in-house digital agencies to assist local businesses with their advertising and marketing needs. All profits made from these new ventures are redeployed to support the journalism in their newspaper – in whatever form it is delivered.

Many of the surviving independent newspapers in the country are family owned and operated, such as the twice-weekly News Reporter in southeastern North Carolina, with a circulation of 10,000. The paper, which serves residents in one of the poorest counties in the state, received the Pulitzer Public Service Medal in 1953 for exposing the infiltration of the Ku Klux Klan into local police and fire departments. Les High, the grandson of that courageous publisher, is now the editor and publisher. He has tried a range of tactics to increase revenue and profitability, including offering videography and web design for local businesses, creating lifestyle magazines and charging for digital subscriptions. He hangs on, despite profit margins in the low single digits, out of a commitment to the community. "The economy, health, education – we know there are a lot of quality-of-life issues here in Columbus that will affect our future," he says. "And if we don't cover them, no one else will."[103]

While most of the third- and fourth-generation family-owned newspapers that have come on the market in recent years have been subsumed by large chains, a small, but growing number have been purchased – at least in part – by local residents who banded together to raise money to keep their hometown paper in local hands. In July 2019, with the support of local residents in Bend, Oregon, EO Media Group purchased the Bend Bulletin and Redmond Spokesman in bankruptcy proceedings for $3.6 million, beating out two out-of-state newspaper chains – Adams Publishing, based in Tennessee, and Rhode Island Suburban Newspapers Inc. (RISN). Executives at the Oregon-based EO Media credited the strong financial support of local residents, including the Bend Foundation, with helping them secure the winning bid. "It's reassuring for the future of community newspapers when a small independent company like EO Media Group can prevail, even when going up against the big companies that are buying up newspapers nonstop around the country," said the EO Media Group chief operating officer, Heidi Wright.[104]

Across the country, in Massachusetts, Fredric Rutberg, a retired judge, joined with three other local residents in 2016 to buy his faltering hometown paper from a large national chain and reinstate local ownership. The local group of investors purchased the Berkshire Eagle in Pittsfield, along with two small dailies and a weekly in neighboring Vermont, from the Digital First newspaper chain, owned by the hedge fund Alden Capital. The new local owners immediately added journalists and marketing staff and invested in both print and digital

upgrades and enhancements, including starting a lifestyle magazine and establishing an in-house digital ad agency. The new owners have had to temper their initial optimism. While circulation of the print newspapers stabilized, there has not been a dramatic uptick. With the coronavirus economic shutdown depressing revenue for the print paper, Rutberg, New England Newspaper's president and publisher, began focusing on launching a locally based philanthropic initiative to support the paper. His advice for those who want to purchase a newspaper: Raise enough money to not only purchase the paper, but also invest in it.[105]

West Virginia University, through its NewStart program, is hoping to inspire a new generation of journalists to buy a local newspaper that serves a marginalized community at risk of becoming a news desert. In April, the NewStart program, created in partnership with the West Virginia Press Association, announced a diverse group of fellows from across the country, the first to participate in an online master's program that provides guidance on developing "new business models during this time of forced innovation."[106]

Giving a Bigger Voice to the New Majority

While independent ownership has been decreasing among community newspapers, a significant demographic shift in this country – propelled by the growth of Hispanic residents – is nurturing exactly the opposite among ethnic news organizations. Independent ownership of minority and ethnic newspapers and magazines, especially, has increased over the past two decades.

Ethnic newspapers have historically been the prime source of relevant news and information for recent immigrants, everything from explaining how to use transportation systems in large cities to exploring big-picture issues, such as criminal justice and discrimination, overlooked by mainstream media. They have been described as "vitamin supplements for their communities and more" that "do not have to apologize to their readers for their social conscience."[107]

Almost 500 of the 950 ethnic news outlets in the UNC database are newspapers. Like many community newspapers, many older, more established ethnic papers are struggling to transform themselves and maintain profitability as print advertising and circulation decline, and younger generations of readers look to more mainstream media outlets and social media for both their news and information. In an attempt to remain relevant and profitable, the Chicago Defender, one of the most influential African-American papers in the 20th century, announced in 2019 that it was discontinuing its print edition, which had only 16,000 subscribers, and moving all its content online, where it reached an average of half a million visitors a month.[108] Older Hispanic newspapers, such as El Diario/La Prensa in New York, are also struggling.[109]

But with the Latino population growing at a rate that surpasses all other white and nonwhite ethnic groups – especially in the South and Southwest – a new generation of owners and titles have gained loyal readers, as well as advertisers who want to pitch their consumer products to first- and second-generation immigrants and their families. There are more than 200 Hispanic newspapers in the UNC database. Many of the "Latino newspapers, news magazines and web-only periodicals are privately held, independent companies, owned by Latino immigrants," according to a recent survey of Latino news media.[110] Many have only one or two people employed in the newsroom and are primarily focused on advocating around specific issues. Others have gained national and regional audiences with their more traditional journalism. Mundo Hispanico, purchased from Cox Media in 2018 by a group of Latino investors, has a print circulation of more than 70,000 that serves more than 200,000 Hispanic residents in the Atlanta metro area. It has also developed a national presence with its website, the third-largest Spanish-speaking site in the country. Under new ownership, and with low overhead, Mundo Hispanico is experimenting with new forms of content – documentaries, as well as

STATES WITH MOST ETHNIC MEDIA

State	Sites
California	142
Texas	94
New York	91
Florida	75
North Carolina	36
Georgia	34
Illinois	32
New Jersey	26
Pennsylvania	22
Ohio	19

expanded sports and food coverage – in an attempt to attract new forms of advertising and sponsorships.[111]

Most of the 173 Hispanic television stations that offer news are owned and managed by large corporations, including Univision and Comcast.[112] However, many of the 37 Latino radio stations that offer news are small and owned by Latino community members. Radio has historically played an important role in reaching not only newly arrived Hispanic immigrants outside of metro areas, but also Native American populations living on reservations, which have very low broadband penetrations. A study by the Democracy Fund found that since 1998 the number of media outlets serving tribal communities has dropped from 700 to 200. "The only bright spot: radio stations increased from 30 to 59 over the past two decades."[113]

In contrast, digital outlets have struggled to gain a foothold in minority and ethnic communities with either readers or advertisers, who have failed to migrate from print and broadcast outlets to websites. A study by the City University of New York (CUNY) counted only 87 digital-only Latino publications, "most of them websites with small or no newsrooms."[114] Many inner-city neighborhoods that are home to some of the largest concentrations of minority and ethnic communities have low broadband penetration and spotty wireless. Flint Beat, established in 2017 by a television reporter in response to the contaminated water crisis in that Michigan city, has struggled to gain an audience, in a city where 40 percent of households live in poverty and do not have internet subscriptions.[115]

Like mainstream commercial television stations and community newspapers, many ethnic news organizations remain overwhelmingly reliant on advertising to support their journalism. With traditional advertising declining, and digital advertising failing to materialize, financial sustainability is a major concern. "Small print publications, including free newspapers that have served local communities for years, are struggling to get ads from the small community-owned businesses that traditionally supported them. … At the same time, the transition to digital platforms, mostly websites, has been challenging, because ad money is not migrating to the publications' online sites." With fewer resources, many struggle to produce original content.[116]

The key challenge for all ethnic media is "to keep the momentum going in a way that allows them to monetize their audience," says Melita Garza, professor at Texas Christian University.[117] Acknowledging the dramatic demographic shifts that will occur in the country's population over the next two decades as the number of nonwhite residents surpasses that of white residents – and the importance of minority and ethnic populations in covering marginalized communities, the CUNY report concludes that the future of ethnic news organizations is "fraught with uncertainty but replete with opportunities."[118]

All Digital All the Time

In February 2019, Kara Meyberg Guzman, who had recently resigned as managing editor of a California paper owned by Digital First because of "differences with the company's management," became her own boss, CEO and co-founder of Santa Cruz Local, a news site covering public policy issues in a city of 65,000 residents. The site was founded as a private, for-profit venture because it was "a quick way to get legal and financial protection" but "the ideals are similar to those of a nonprofit … to contribute to the greater good." Incorporating as a for-profit site also allowed the founders to weigh in on elections and endorse candidates for office, which nonprofit sites are not permitted to do.[119]

Roughly half of the 525 independent local sites in the UNC database are for-profit enterprises, although many, like Santa Cruz Local, also seek and accept grants from foundations and individuals. More than three-quarters of those sites focus on providing very local news, including coverage of routine government meetings, with the remainder tackling broad regional and statewide issues, such as education or politics. Many have been established by experienced and passionate journalists, like Guzman, who spotted a critical information need. While the number of newspaper journalists declined by 36,000 since 2008, the overall number of journalists employed in digital newsrooms has increased by 10,000.[120]

Digital journalists can have a significant impact on the quality of news and information available to residents in a community. A recent study by Duke University found that online-only media outlets were a relatively small component of the overall media mix, accounting for only about 10 percent of the 16,000 stories produced in news outlets in a hundred cities (ranging in size from 20,000 to 300,000) in a typical week. Nevertheless, 80 percent of the stories produced by digital sites addressed one of the critical information needs identified by the Federal Communications Commission – on topics such as education, health, the environment or local governance and politics.[121]

Yet, despite the best of journalistic intentions, many of the founders of these independent sites are struggling to gain a toehold in the market where they are located and produce enough income to achieve long-term financial security. Although 83 new local sites were added to the UNC database in 2019, an equal number disappeared, as sites that were active in 2018 went dormant. A Los Angeles Times study in 2015 found that one in four local digital sites failed within five years.[122]

Most of the sites in the UNC database – 90 percent – are located in metro areas, where there is more access to both for-profit and nonprofit funding, but also much more competition from other media, including other digital sites, as well as radio, television and well-established print publications, including magazines and newspapers. This can make it very hard to gain traction and attract enough revenue from subscribers, sponsors or advertisers to support expansion of news coverage. As a result, many of the online sites have only a couple of journalists on staff.

With very small staffs, most of the local digital sites are also constrained in their ability to provide a consistent supply of relevant news and information – especially to residents outside the major metro area. Additionally, most are located in affluent communities that tend to vote Democratic and not in economically struggling communities that voted Republican in 2016. Only three are located in the 200 counties that have lost a newspaper, including the Orleans Hub in upstate New York, and Mahoning Matters, a joint venture of McClatchy and Google, located in Youngstown, Ohio. When the Washington Post closed The Gazette in Montgomery County, Maryland, in 2015, the founder of Maryland Reporter, a digital newsletter that covers state government and politics, "spent a few weeks researching the possibilities for a nonprofit news website in Montgomery County," the state's largest county with a million residents. But he concluded "that I had neither the time or the energy to get such a site funded."[123]

As newspapers continue to struggle and disappear, the Local Independent Online News (LION) association, established in 2012, is hoping it can provide resources that will allow entrepreneurial journalists to establish websites that fill the information void, while also achieving long-term financial security. LION has some 260 members, 65 percent of which are for-profit. "There are a ton of reporting and editing and writing resources out there for reporters," says Anika Anand, founder of Evergrey in Seattle, part of the WhereBy.Us network. "But it is much harder to find resources around revenue and operations." With funding from two large grants received in 2019 and 2020, LION is hoping to provide the founders of digital sites with the resources to achieve long-term financial sustainability. It is creating a "tech starter pack" and enlisting a stable of consultants for both members and aspiring founders, so local publishers don't have to make decisions "semi-blindly on their own."[124]

Many of the early local news sites established between 2008 and 2012 envisioned a business model that relied primarily on digital revenue from local business. Robert Chappell, founder of Madison365, a local nonprofit news site in Wisconsin's state capital, believes, "Local news can work as a business when it's not owned by venture capital."[125] However, as prospects of garnering enough revenue from digital advertising have diminished in recent years, many websites, even for-profit ones, are increasingly looking to the nonprofit world to supply those funds.

THE NONPROFIT MODEL:
Increasingly Important for Newsrooms

Nonprofit dollars have nurtured the success of magazines, such as Consumer Reports and Harper's, as well as a small number of newspapers – including the Tampa Bay Times and The Citizen in Charlotte, Vermont – for decades. However, the rapid collapse of the for-profit business model that historically supported local newsgathering has prompted renewed interest in nonprofit funding of local news sites, as well as local newspapers, including The Salt Lake Tribune, which sought and received nonprofit tax status in 2019, allowing the paper to establish a foundation to accept donations.

ProPublica and The Texas Tribune, established in 2007 and 2009, demonstrated that, with the support of deep-pocketed individual donors and foundations, it was possible for national and regional sites to achieve long-term sustainability. More recently, local and regional sites – such as Charlottesville Tomorrow in Virginia and VTDigger in Vermont – have been experimenting with nonprofit models that work on a smaller regional scale. Since 2008, nonprofit newsrooms have launched at an

average of one a month, according to the Institute for Nonprofit News (INN), which counts 250 members. Half of the INN member sites cover state and local news. Almost all the sites pursue a civic mission of providing investigative and explanatory journalism. Eighty percent of the sites have at least one investigative reporter, while 70 percent filed open records requests in 2018.[126]

Despite the rate at which nonprofit newsrooms have been launched, there is still a gap in the funding needed to support the establishment of new sites, especially in economically struggling communities that are most likely to be at risk of becoming news deserts. A 2018 report by the Shorenstein Center at Harvard's Kennedy School pointed out the challenges. It noted that many large national and community foundations did not realize "just how much of the newspaper and commercial media workforce has been lost and why that matters." As a result, local and state news organizations received only about 5 percent – or $80 million – of the $1.8 billion in journalism-related grants made by more than 6,500

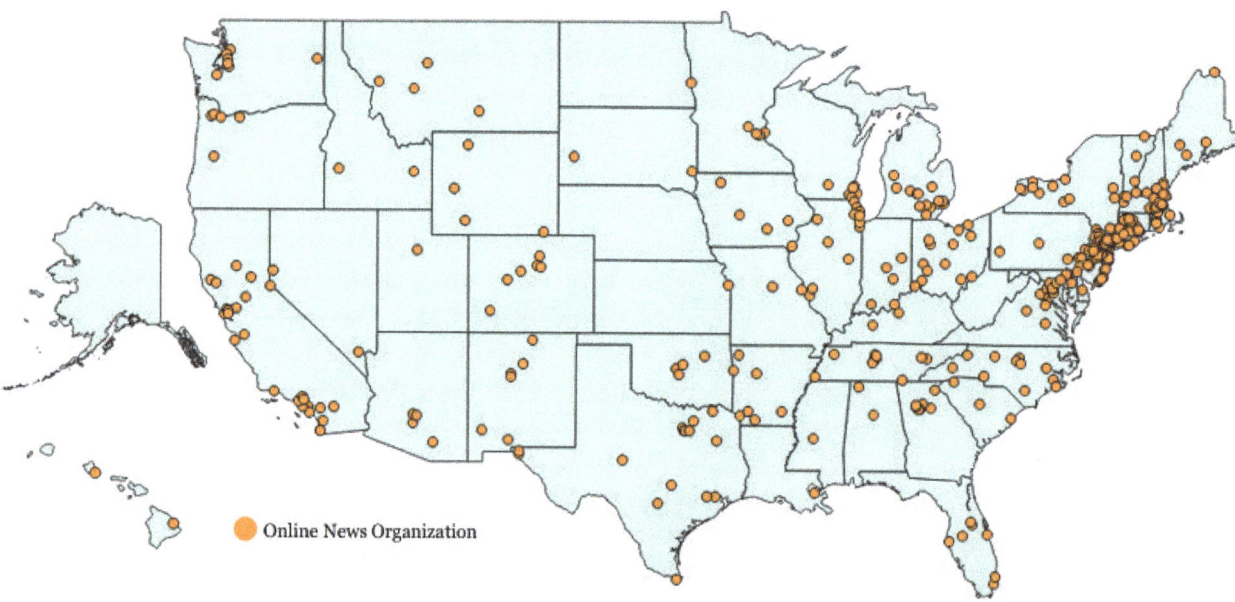

IS DIGITAL FILLING THE VOID?

● Online News Organization

While the U.S. has lost more than 2,100 newspapers, only about 500 local or state digital news sites have filled the void.

Source: Local Independent Online News (LION) Publishers, OASIS Project

foundations between 2010 and 2015. Furthermore, the study found local and state news nonprofits also depended on a very limited pool of foundations for their support, with the Knight Foundation accounting for 20 percent of all funding of news organizations.[127]

Concerned over the state of local news, in 2019, the Knight Foundation pledged $300 million over five years to support local news initiatives and has encouraged other foundations to increase their funding.[128] But many of the foundations with large endowments, by tradition and mission, have prioritized specific causes and missions unrelated to journalism, such as the arts, economic development, social justice or health. Changing the philanthropic priorities of a foundation presents considerable institutional obstacles that involve agreement among major stakeholders and board members. The majority of the annual income that the foundations' endowments produce – as much as 90 percent – may have already been designated for a specific purpose, leaving the foundation managers with little flexibility to redirect funds to local news. Finally, there is also a disparity between the endowments of many community funds in large metro areas compared with those in small and mid-sized communities. The Cleveland Foundation, for example has an endowment of more than $13.5 billion, while the Mahoning Valley Foundation, based in Youngstown, Ohio, which lost its daily newspaper, The Vindicator, in 2019, has an endowment of only $65 million.[129]

The Shorenstein report also noted the disparity between a dozen or so news sites that received substantial funding from major foundations compared with the vast majority of nonprofit newsrooms that received much smaller grants, often only enough to support a specific reporting project. Large grants from foundations are important, the report noted, because they provide news organizations with the financial wherewithal to ramp up their journalism in their early years and gain support from sustaining individual donors. Without an initial large grant, many founders of smaller nonprofit sites reported that they were forced to continually fundraise. In 2016, even the smallest of nonprofit news organizations relied on foundations – both large family and community ones and small community-based ones – for two-thirds of their funding.[130]

This has led to an aggressive effort in recent years by nonprofits to diversify their income sources. The 2019

survey of INN members found that 40 percent had developed four or more sources of funding, including individual donations, corporate sponsorships and syndication of content. With training on how to engage communities, the INN organizations have managed to increase donations from individuals to 39 percent of the total $450 million in revenue raised in 2019, while foundation funding had decreased to 43 percent from two-thirds in 2016. However, only 10 percent came from reader subscriptions or memberships, and two-thirds of those donors were deep-pocketed individual philanthropists, who contributed more than $5,000 each. This meant that most INN nonprofit news sites today still rely on either large grants from foundations or large donations from individuals for the majority – 80 percent – of their annual budget and for their long-term sustainability.[131]

While almost 40 percent of INN's nonprofit newsrooms generated more than $1 million in 2018, a third generated less than $250,000. With nonprofit funding in limited supply, significant grants often involve collaborations – among foundations and individuals with specific interests, and among for-profit and nonprofit news organizations. The Wichita Community Foundation, for example, is funding a journalistic collaboration among 11 news organizations – including the local newspaper, the NPR and commercial television affiliates, and various niche publications – to examine and report on the causes for the increased suicide rate in Kansas, one of the highest in the country.[132]

"Local [nonprofit] news organizations are networked with, or even part of, regional and national [for-profit and publicly funded] organizations," said Sue Cross, CEO and executive director of INN, "Many more local news organizations will form, but others will merge or team up. So we focus less on the number of separate [nonprofit] news companies and more on the total reporting force they support, in whatever form or set of alliances proves best at supporting robust public service reporting."[133]

INN says its 230 sites currently have 3,000 employees, with 2,000 being journalists. INN's goal is to drive a tenfold increase over the coming decade "and grow the field to a network of at least 20,000 nonprofit journalists by 2030," Cross said. "That would give the country a new backbone of civic coverage spanning local news, state coverage and national investigative and expert beat reporting."[134]

THE PUBLICLY FUNDED MODEL:
Over the Air and Streaming

For many residents living in communities without newspapers and without easy access to high-speed internet, the primary source for local news is either the television or radio station. In 2019, slightly more than a third of American residents said they relied on local and regional television stations as the primary source of their local news, down from 47 percent in 2016. As many as a fourth of residents in small and mid-sized markets outside metro areas said they regularly listened to news radio.[135]

When watching television news, residents are most likely tuning to one of more than 820 commercial stations, instead of the nation's 169 public broadcasting television stations. With radio, they are most likely relying on one of 1,100 public radio stations affiliated with either NPR or American Public Media, instead of the more than 10,000 commercial stations.[136] As viewership of local commercial television newscasts has declined in recent years – and local newspapers have disappeared – policymakers have begun to revisit the mission of public broadcasting and question whether more funding and programming on public television and radio should be dedicated to local news.

The country's public broadcasting system, which is 53 years old in 2020, is a relative newcomer compared with commercial broadcasting in the United States, which dates back a century. It was set up in a time when television entertainment and cultural programming was in the early stages of its existence, with only three commercial networks. The PBS stations were established to address what was perceived as a deficit in educational programming, such as "Sesame Street," and cultural programming, such as "Masterpiece Theatre." NPR was offered several years later "as a sort of after-thought."[137]

Federal funding of public broadcasting has been relatively level in recent years. In 2019, Congress allocated $447 million to fund the Corporation for Public Broadcasting, of which two-thirds ($298 million) went for programming and

staffing at PBS stations, and slightly more than one-fifth ($99 million) went to NPR stations.[138] Depending on the station, federal funds amounted to between 20 and 40 percent of total revenue, with most of the rest coming from individual giving (40 percent at PBS and 60 percent at NPR) and corporate sponsorships. But most of the government funds – especially at PBS stations – continue to be used for entertainment and news programs that attract a national audience, even though many of those entertainment programs are now offered on multiple platforms, including Amazon and Netflix.[139]

Only 13 of 169 PBS stations – ranging from WNET in New York to WVUT in Vincennes, Indiana, the smallest station – produce four or more daily local news shows each week. There is an average of four full-time journalists per PBS station, with the majority covering national news. In contrast, the country's 820 commercial television stations that offer news programming employ an average of 35 to 40 per station, almost all focused on state and local news.[140]

As a result, both critics and champions of public broadcasting invariably look to the recent success of NPR – not PBS – as a potential roadmap for revitalizing local news on public television and expanding the news coverage on radio. "NPR stations in Boston, New York, San Francisco, St. Louis and Dallas have become local news powerhouses," producing both expansive local coverage of news and investigative and exploratory journalism.[141]

At the national level, the total operating budget for NPR in 2018 was $252.1 million – less than the amount PBS receives from government funding alone. While 69 percent of the 1,100 public radio stations report that they offer "local news," Robert Papper, who is director of the annual survey conducted by the Radio Television Digital News Association (RTDNA), points out that not all of these stations have reporters that "cover" or "gather" the news.[142] Rather they employ hosts and moderators of

TOP 16 STATES WITH PUBLIC BROADCASTING OUTLETS

State	NPR	PBS	APM	APM/NPR	Pacifica	Total
USA	1047	346	49	39	4	1485
Minnesota	12	10	44	25		91
California	59	13	2	4	2	80
New York	70	10				80
Texas	40	12			1	53
Alaska	46	4				50
Colorado	42	6				48
Oregon	40	7				47
Ohio	31	12				43
Wisconsin	35	8				43
Michigan	30	10		1		41
North Carolina	28	13				41
Virginia	34	7				41
Washington	33	7				40
Florida	14	21				35
Iowa	23	9	1	2		35
Illinois	25	10				35

Source: UNC Database

news shows, who interview experts and other journalists who have reported on the breaking news story for another news outlets.

Since the 3,000 journalists employed by NPR represent less than 10 percent of the 34,000 newspaper journalists lost over the past decade, NPR reporters have to pool resources and be selective about which stories they cover. Wisconsin Public Radio in Madison has created a loose beat system, assigning different specialties to different stations – for example, agriculture to a station in the western part of the state on the Minnesota border.[143] The Kansas News Service draws on the talent at three NPR stations in Kansas, plus one in Kansas City, Missouri. Three fulltime and two part-time journalists provide coverage of the state legislature, as well as in-depth coverage of the environment and education.[144]

NPR stations in both Texas and California have formed collaborations that produce big projects and daily newscasts. The Texas Newsroom, which launched in 2019, produces six weekday statewide newscasts that draw content from public radio stations across the state. The California Dream project, a collaboration of five public radio stations, produced a series of stories in 2019 on issues of economic opportunity and disparity in the state. In 2020, the same California stations are teaming up to focus on "boost reporting from and for underserved regions across the state."[145]

National public radio is available to 95 percent of the country, including areas that do not have high broadband penetration. Especially in more remote small and mid-sized markets, radio is critical in local news. Both Wisconsin and Vermont Public Radio have a goal of employing a journalist

in every county in their states.[146] But current funding –
from both the government and the nonprofit world – can
only be stretched so far. In his annual survey of radio
stations for the Radio Television Digital News Association
(RTDNA), Syracuse University professor Robert Papper
found that the "number one concern" of both commercial
and public radio was "financial sustainability."[147] Even with
a reporter in every county, Noah Ovshinsky, news director
at Wisconsin Public Radio, is "skeptical that we can fill that
vacuum" left when a community loses a newspapers. "That
would be a pretty big ask," given current funds."[148]

The 2018 report by Harvard's Shorenstein Center noted
that two-thirds of the $795 million in grants from
foundations in 2016 went to 25 public broadcasting
stations in 10 states.[149] "Such concentration means that
public media organizations across the great majority of

states lack the foundation funding necessary to evolve
into central hubs for local and state news reporting, filling
gaps in newspaper coverage and nurturing other local
news nonprofits," it concludes.

Howard Husock, who served on the board of the
Corporation for Public Broadcasting from 2013 to 2018,
is calling for "a new Carnegie Commission" that would
explore ways to re-evaluate the role of public media in
producing more local news. Among the questions he
suggests exploring: Does it still make sense to prioritize
investments in over-the-air infrastructure, or would
rural broadband be the appropriate successor? Should
the bulk of funding still be dedicated to television, the
most expensive form of production? How can public
media better reflect the country's full range of cultures
and viewpoints?[150]

THE LESSONS LEARNED: 2004 TO 2019

Approximately 1,800 of the 2,100 communities that have lost a newspaper since 2004 do not have another nearby news outlet covering issues of very local concern – such as the quality of schools in that community or the spread of an infectious disease. Without a journalist covering school board meetings, vetting candidates for local office and covering everyday events and celebrations, residents in thousands of small and mid-sized communities are living in a news desert, without access to reliable information about important issues that can determine the quality of their lives now and in the future. Most of these communities are struggling economically. Many also lack the technological infrastructure, such as high-speed internet, that facilitates communication of news and information in the 21st century.

As local newspapers vanished, numerous rounds of layoffs simultaneously depleted the reporting and editing staffs at the nation's metro and state dailies. Although journalists at other media outlets – digital sites, public broadcasting outlets, regional television stations and ethnic media – have attempted to step into the breach, their efforts have failed to significantly reverse the trend.

In 2020, there were many fewer journalists covering important routine government meetings in small and mid-sized markets or producing major investigative and analytical pieces on state and regional papers that held government officials accountable. Most digital sites, ethnic news organizations and public broadcasting outlets have only a handful of journalists on staff. And most are located in major metro areas, where they have more access to funds, but are constrained in their ability to provide comprehensive and consistent news coverage to underserved communities – inner-city neighborhoods, outlying suburbs and rural communities that have lost their hometown paper.

Most local news organizations – whether for-profit, nonprofit or publicly funded – are small businesses, and cash is the currency of small business. They tend to operate month-to-month, or quarter-to-quarter, without significant cash reserves. A bad quarter can sink them financially. All news organizations – the surviving newspapers, digital sites, ethnic media organizations and public broadcasting outlets – are struggling to transform their business models to meet the challenges of the digital age. The savviest entrepreneurs are constantly seeking ways to engage new audiences and diversify their income. But they need money to innovate, and that has been in short supply.

A journal article in 2009 surveyed the rapidly changing media landscape and asked whether news organizations of the future would be transformed or diminished.[151] In 2019, it is apparent the local news ecosystem is *both* transformed and diminished. The current demand – *and critical need* – for local news outstrips the supply.

From 1990 to 1999, the Public Service Medal, the most prestigious Pulitzer Prize, was awarded, in unprecedented fashion, to three small, but mighty newspapers: The Washington Daily News in North Carolina, for "revealing that the city's water supply was contaminated with carcinogens." The Virgin Island Daily News, "for its disclosure of the links between the region's rampant crime rate and corruption in the local criminal justice system." And the Grand Forks Herald in North Dakota, "for its sustained and informative coverage … in the wake of flooding, a blizzard and a fire that devastated much of the city, including the newspaper plant itself."[152]

The coronavirus pandemic has reminded us, yet again, of the vital importance of local news. Interest in and appreciation for local news has surged in recent months, as residents in cities and rural communities have searched for accurate, reliable and comprehensive information about what is occurring in their own neighborhood. Yet, at this very moment, local news organizations, large and small, for-profit and nonprofit, are confronting a dire economic threat to their existence.

Even in their drastically diminished state, surviving local newspapers still remain a vital source of local news and information. A recent study found that local newspapers produce more than half of all original local stories that address a critical information need – such as education, the environment and the health and safety of our community. This suggests the importance of public policy and philanthropic efforts that support the viability of strong local newspapers, as well as digital-only news outlets, ethnic media and public broadcasting. In order to replenish and revive the local news ecosystem, and address the information needs of underserved communities, there needs to be both a significant increase in funding and a recommitment to journalism's civic mission.

THE NEWS LANDSCAPE OF THE FUTURE: TRANSFORMED. . . AND RENEWED?

An ecosystem is often very fragile. The slightest disruption can lead to adaptive evolution and renewal, or diminishment and demise. It is too early to know which local news organizations will have the fortitude and good fortune to emerge from the economic collapse of 2020 in a position to thrive in the years ahead. But it is not difficult to discern the underlying challenges and opportunities local news organizations will face in this decade and the next. If we are to thwart the continued rise of news deserts across this country, we need to reimagine the journalistic mission and business model for local news, use technology to develop new capabilities and craft new policies that address disparities that have given rise to news deserts.

We know the demographics of this nation are changing. Sometime in the fourth decade of this century, minority populations – African Americans, Hispanics, Native Americans and Asian Americans – will surpass the number of whites of European heritage living in the United States. Intentionally and unintentionally, traditional local news organizations – local newspapers, as well as television and radio stations and start-up digital outlets – have often overlooked and disenfranchised minority populations, who have turned instead to their own minority-owned media. How does the journalistic mission of both mainstream news outlets and ethnic media – often considered "niche" – change, and potentially converge, when the minorities become a majority?

We know the business model that historically sustained local news organizations is broken and must be rebuilt. More than $37 billion in annual print revenue alone has disappeared over the past 15 years, as advertisers followed consumers and moved online. During that same time, the nation has lost a fourth of its local newspapers and more than half of the journalists employed by newspapers, leaving residents in entire communities without access to credible and comprehensive news coverage of their everyday lives, as well as historic events. Despite the efforts of entrepreneurs to close the gap, news deserts are spreading inexorably across the continent. Invariably the communities most at risk are those that are economically struggling and bypassed by the digital age. Leaving these communities isolated and cut off risks further polarization of this country. Reversing the trend will require deployment of a variety of business models. To reinvigorate the local news ecosystem, there will need to be a dramatic increase in funding for local news from corporations and businesses, news consumers, financiers, philanthropists and taxpayers.

Digital technology has revolutionized the way we think about producing, consuming and delivering news, yet news organizations have only begun to explore the potential and come face-to-face with the unintended consequences. Technology can connect news organizations with disenfranchised communities, but the content on its platforms can also divide a nation. It can be used by journalists to sift and sort complicated databases and enlighten the public about issues bubbling just below the surface. Alternatively, the information mined can also obfuscate the obvious. Most media companies are organized around "content as king." Most tech companies are organized around the aggregation and distribution of content created by someone else. Utilizing artificial intelligence to reach new audiences and enhance journalism will require a collaboration between the major tech companies and news organizations that does not yet exist.

Finally, all of this requires a rethinking of policies and regulations at the national, state and local levels. It is about more than antitrust legislation or cross-ownership rules, the big issues in the 20th century. It is about tackling questions such as: How big is too big – for both start-up tech companies and legacy media enterprises? How do you encourage local ownership of news organizations? Is there a societal benefit, as well an economic benefit, to revisiting cross-ownership rules? Do local newspapers deserve special protection, since they are still a vital source of local news for most communities? How do you combat misinformation? How do you deliver the news to communities that are on the margins? How do you encourage diversity of voices and perspectives? What is the responsibility of tech companies in curating and delivering the news? How do you pay for journalism in the digital age? And who should pay more – taxpayers, giant tech companies, media corporations, subscribers or deep-pocketed individual donors, philanthropic organizations, or all of the above?

This is a pivotal moment – for thousands of local news organizations struggling to adapt to new economic and digital realities, as well as dealing with the unforeseen consequences of a technological revolution that has exacerbated political, social and economic divisions among citizens of this country. This section anticipates the future by exploring what we know today about the challenges and opportunities we're confronting:

Journalistic Mission

For decades, ethnic and minority media have focused on providing their audiences with critical information that was not provided by more mainstream outlets. In our 2020 report, UNC has begun compiling a list of more than 950 minority and ethnic media outlets, separate from the list of print, broadcasting and digital news organizations. What lessons do ethnic media offer in terms of engaging and covering disenfranchised communities and marginalized populations? What issues will they confront in the near future as the country's minority populations become the majority?

Business Model

In contrast to many European countries, the United States allocates only a fraction of taxpayer money to support news programming on its 1,400 public radio and television stations. Given the financial challenges confronting local news organizations, does our nation need to consider significantly increasing public funding for them? What topics and communities do PBS and NPR cover now? What is missing? Where could additional public funding make the biggest difference?

Technological Capabilities

Facebook has unveiled several initiatives and products over the past two years designed to combat the rise of news deserts. A product called *Today In* … (followed by the name of the city, such as *Today in Raleigh*) is available in thousands of communities in 2020. UNC researchers explored the type and timeliness of local news the *Today In* algorithm chose for North Carolina residents over the past year. Algorithms are already being used by some news organizations to compose simple news stories. What happens when algorithms alone are curators and editors of our local news?

Policies and Regulations

Over the past decade, various policies and regulations that were designed to support local news encountered either opposition or apathy. One benefit of the coronavirus pandemic is that it has focused attention on the vital importance of accurate and timely local news and information while also exposing the fragility of the news ecosystem. As a result, for the first time, there is bipartisan support in Congress for addressing at least some of the most pressing issues. This section explores current legislation and policies being considered at both the national and state levels.

This report concludes with a simple exercise, **Rate Your Local News**, that allows you to judge the quantity and quality of news in your own community. What outlets are providing you with news you can actually use? How much of it is locally produced? What is missing from your daily diet? Understanding the current state of local news in your own community is vital in charting a path forward.

JOURNALISTIC MISSION:
The Challenges and Opportunities for Ethnic Media

As many mainstream news outlets disappear, some areas of the United States have seen an explosion in new media offerings aimed at various ethnic groups, reflecting the nation's changing demographics. By 2045, the U.S. Census Bureau estimates that non–Hispanic whites will be outnumbered by the current minority population, composed primarily of African Americans, Native Americans, Asian Americans and Latinos.[153] This suggests a broader journalistic mission for ethnic media in the coming decades. UNC identified 950 ethnic news outlets in the country in 2020. Researchers Bill Arthur and Jeremiah Murphy examine the state of ethnic media in America.

As the makeup of the country's population changes, ethnic news outlets are playing a key role in providing essential news to groups of people who often get scant attention in the mainstream press. "News deserts are not only geographic," says Madeleine Bair, founder of El Tímpano, who spent nine months researching the information needs of the Spanish-speaking residents of Oakland, California, before launching her publication. "Local news outlets certainly cover a local community, but they don't necessarily cover or serve all communities within that geography."

Ethnic media publications cover a wide range of nationalities, cultures, languages and generations. Some publications, like the 145-year-old African American Savannah Tribune or the Native American Navajo Times, reach out to more established communities, while newer Latino news outlets, such as North Carolina's La Noticia, target newly arrived Hispanic residents in that state. "With ethnic media, you have the niche of the niche," says Sandy Close, founder and director of the San Francisco-based Ethnic Media Services, which works to foster and sustain ethnic news outlets. "You can't get more local."

These news outlets cover issues of daily importance like schools and local politics, as well as the specific health issues affecting their communities.[154] "In the best case, we are undercovered. In the worst case, we are ignored," says Hilda Gurdian, La Noticia's publisher. "People watch our news in order to survive in this country," said Univision anchor Jorge Ramos in a recent American Press Institute article. "We are providing essential information. ... How does one receive a scholarship, how does one get medical insurance, how to vote on the day of elections."[155]

More than information, ethnic news outlets offer a counter-narrative to the mainstream. "The Black press was never intended to be objective, because it didn't see the white press being objective," Phyllis Garland, the first African American to be a tenured faculty member at the Columbia University Graduate School of Journalism, said in a 1999 documentary.[156]

Like the mainstream media, many ethnic media outlets are struggling to stay profitable, but they also face specific issues that make the larger challenges all that more difficult. Not surprisingly, the biggest growth in ethnic news outlets has occurred in the states with the largest minority populations. Here is the current state of ethnic media, based on analysis of the 951 ethnic news outlets identified by UNC:

- California has the most ethnic media outlets (142), followed by Texas (96), New York (91) and Florida (76). California and Texas have minority populations that in total outnumber the white, non-Hispanic population. Florida and New York have minority populations of 46 percent.[157]

- The overwhelming majority of ethnic media outlets are in urban areas, suggesting that growing communities in rural areas are underserved.[158]

- The largest number of ethnic news outlets are aimed at Latin-Hispanic communities, which are growing at a rate that eclipses all other groups, even though immigration from Latino countries is down in recent years. A Pew Research Center study found 224 Latino-Hispanic newspapers, 173 TV stations and 27 radio stations.

- The African American population is served by 243 newspapers, 28 radio stations and seven TV stations. While the African American population growth hasn't increased like the Latino community, there has been a sharp increase in immigrants from African countries, according to Pew.[159]

- Some 35 news outlets in the UNC database serve the Asian American community, and 10 more are aimed at Native Americans. Other communities, Polish, German, Italian, Russian and others, are served by 67 outlets.

- Ethnic media outlets are mostly independent businesses, with the exception of a few conglomerates such as Entravision Communications (28 Hispanic/Latino outlets), NBC Universal (26 Hispanic/Latino Outlets) and Univision (20 Hispanic/Latino outlets). Independent news outlets – such as the newspaper the Weekly Bangalee, the "AfroLatino Podcast" Afrosaya and the 100-year-old Japanese newspaper RafuShimpo – face the same business challenges as mainstream outlets: how to make money and stay in business.

- Ethnic media is most often presented in the language of the target audience – Spanish, Chinese, Vietnamese. In general, first-generation immigrants tend to rely on receiving information from newspapers, television and radio in their native language.

- Like most news outlets, ethnic media publications are increasingly experimenting with delivering news beyond traditional print formats. El Tímpano uses, text alerts to provide timely information, both for news and for emergencies like wildfires. "People want to know, is it safe for children to be outside?" says Bair, the El Tímpano founder.

The Business of Ethnic Media

Print and television are still heavyweights in ethnic media, with digital and mobile platforms growing quickly. Some ethnic news outlets are large, such as African-American News & Issues, a minority, woman-owned weekly that claims a distribution of 113,000 in Texas. Some are corporate owned, such as Gannett's La Voz in Phoenix, Arizona, which distributes 60,000 free copies of its newspaper to racks in grocery stores, shopping centers and restaurants every Friday. Others are small start-ups whose owners include "a full-time musician, a used-car salesman, an immigration lawyer and an assistant teacher,"[160] who use income from their "day jobs" to support their news operations.

Advertising is the main source of revenue for most of these outlets and is as much a source in crisis for ethnic media as it is for the nation's mainstream news media. African American news outlets were particularly hard hit in the 2008 recession. "When the car dealers and airlines stopped advertising, we lost huge amounts of revenue," says Frances Jackson, publisher of The Chicago Defender, one of the most influential African American newspapers through much of the 20th century.[161] African American newspapers also suffered when tobacco companies stopped their print advertising – Philip Morris in 2004, followed by R.J. Reynolds in 2008. "Cigarettes as well as alcohol, both of those, hit us pretty hard, because they were big advertisers," says Gerald Johnson, publisher of the African American newspaper The Charlotte Post.

Several factors make the ad dollar harder to get for many ethnic media outlets. They frequently have smaller audiences than mainstream counterparts and can't charge as much for ads. Historically, many ethnic outlets have not been audited by independent organizations examining their circulation and ratings,[162] which also makes advertisers reluctant to buy space and time in them. Some advertisers have been slow to recognize the buying power of ethnic communities. The result is that many large national advertisers have overlooked ethnic outlets, forcing them to rely more on "mom and pop" advertisers.[163]

Still, these outlets reach audiences that English language publications do not, so some advertisers seek them out. "We get them the results that they want," La Noticia's Gurdian says. She estimates the buying power of the Latino community in North Carolina at $14 billion. "They are consumers, the same as everybody else."[164]

Many ethnic news outlets, such as the century-old New York Amsterdam News and the 86-year-old Los Angeles Sentinel, have a significant digital presence, supplementing print revenue with online advertising and subscription plans. The Sentinel is available on its website, as an e-newspaper, as an e-blast and on a Sentinel mobile app as well as in print.[165]

The Chicago Defender, 115 years old, is now all digital; it ended its print edition in 2019.[166] But going digital presents its own problems. While digital ad revenue has been increasing across the industry, it hasn't often benefited many ethnic news outlets. Some observers say that as much as 85 percent of new digital ad revenue goes to Facebook and Google.[167] In addition, digital advertising sells for far less than print advertising.

"It's nowhere at the level of revenue" that outlets gained from print and broadcast ads, says Close of **Ethnic Media Services**. Consequently, many outlets have turned to pay walls, or digital subscriptions, for revenue. But except for some esoteric publications aimed at small, select audiences, subscriptions rarely produce enough revenue to keep a publication going. And subscriptions can be a problem for ethnic outlets, whose readers are often on the lower end of the income scale. Median individual income in 2018 was $31,000 for African Americans and $28,000 for Hispanics, compared with $44,803 for white, non-Hispanics.[168]

Then, too, people have been used to getting information for free on Facebook, Twitter or other social media. "Consumers of news, they're so used to getting everything for free that they don't want to pay to be subscribers," Jennifer Parker, editor and publisher of CrossRoadsNews in Decatur, Georgia, said in a 2019 interview with the Medill News Leaders Project. CrossRoadsNews ended its weekly print edition in 2018.

Some ethnic outlets have turned to grants and funding from corporations, charitable foundations or even local governments to run operations. However, ethnic media outlets received only 2.1 percent of the total funding that philanthropic foundations gave all local media outlets from 2010–2015, according to the Shorenstein

WHERE ARE THE ETHNIC VOICES?

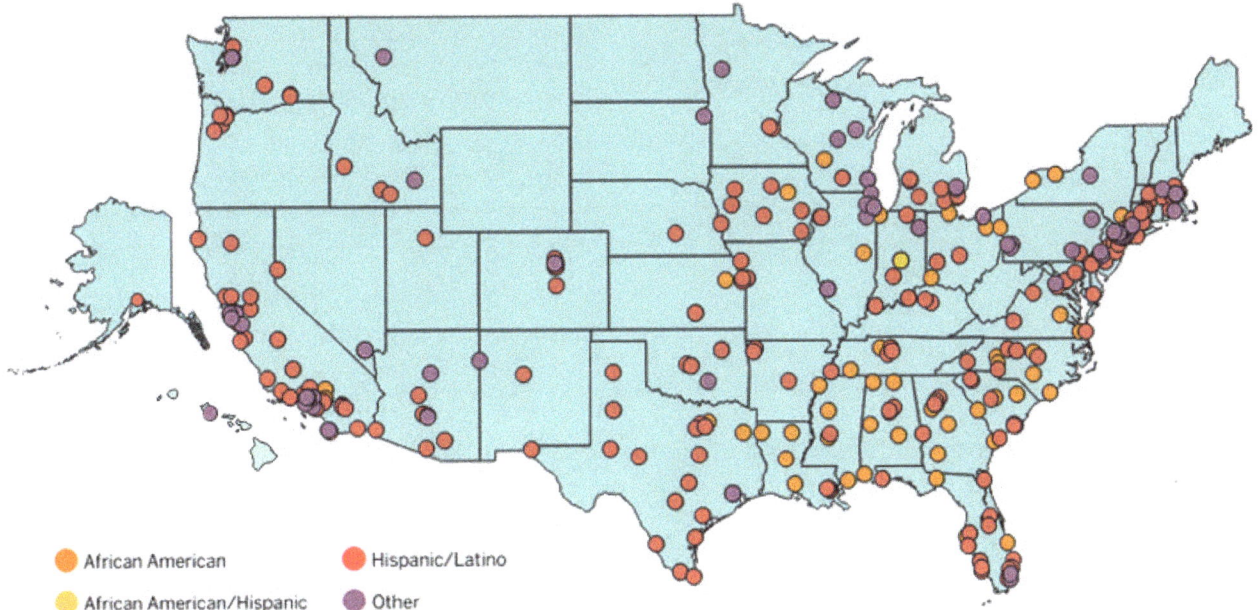

- African American
- African American/Hispanic
- Hispanic/Latino
- Other

There are about 1,000 ethnic media outlets in the country providing news to underserved communities.

Source: UNC Hussman School of Journalism and Media

> *"I really believe the African American community is at the forefront of re-creating who we are as a country."*

Center on Media, Politics and Public Policy at Harvard University.[169] Also, reliance on such funding can leave a news organization beholden to its sponsor. The Democracy Fund reports that Native American "tribes own and mostly control 72 percent of all native print and radio operations in the United States."[170] The result is that Native American media outlets are often perceived to be agents of the tribal government rather than unbiased chroniclers holding those governments accountable to the communities they serve, the fund said.[171]

Other ethnic media outlets receive funding by being a "sister publication" to a mainstream outlet – where both papers share the same owner and some resources. Two examples are El Nuevo Herald with The Miami Herald and Al Día with The Dallas Morning News. The City University of New York writes that this type of relationship often means that Spanish language news isn't a priority: "Editors are often asked to translate content from the English publication into Spanish to fill the pages of the publications for the Latino readers but rarely get their own, original, content translated into English," the CUNY report said.[172]

Also a possibility are mergers and cooperative agreements, such as ImpreMedia's purchase of the Spanish language daily Hoy New York from Tribune Co. in 2007[173] and the Baltimore and Washington Afro-American papers combining their printing operations in 2015.[174] However, mergers and acquisitions can also lead to closures. ImpreMedia shut down Hoy New York in 2009, and the Tribune Publishing Co. closed Hoy in Chicago in late 2019.[175]

By necessity, ethnic media outlets are trying new ways to produce revenue. Sandy Close says one Northern California publication told its staff to work from home and rented out the first floor of its building to pay printing costs. Many outlets have added event planning to their business models. Event planners "want to develop events and develop traditional experiences for the African American community, but they just don't know how to do it, and they don't want to be offensive in the kind of things that they create, so they hire us," Hiram

Jackson, chief executive officer of Real Times Media, the parent company of the Chicago Defender, said in an interview with the Medill Local News Initiative.[176]

The expanding digital landscape also offers other opportunities for innovation. To enlarge its audience to English speakers, Radio Ambulante, a podcast that tells long-form stories about the Latino experience, created an app, Lupa, that teaches people Spanish while they listen to episodes. The app generates revenue through subscriptions, monetizing the opportunity to bridge Spanish-speaking and non-Spanish-speaking listeners.[177]

Ethnic Media's Value: Past, Present and Future

Spanish language media has been with the United States since before the country began. Print news first hit the New World in 1541 – in the form of a single-issue Spanish-language publication detailing the effects of a Guatemalan earthquake. The first published periodical in North America was the Mercurio Volante, published in Mexico in 1693, beating The Boston News-Letter, the first English-language periodical in North America, by 11 years.[178] "Journalism in the Americas thus began in Mexico, when it was joined politically to the area from South Carolina to the Florida peninsula and west to the California coast as part of the Spanish Empire," write historians Nicolás Kanellos and Helvetia Martell.[179]

The first Spanish-language newspaper in the United States was El Misisipí, published in 1808, followed by El Mensajero Luisianés in 1809. The Spanish-language press would go on to serve many communities; first, long-standing native Hispanic communities and then immigrants recently arrived in the U.S. In addition, the Hispanic community is composed of people from different countries with different customs and Spanish vernacular. "Hispanic communities in the United States have been segmented among ethnic, nationality, class and religious lines almost from the beginning," Kanellos and Martell write.

The first African American newspaper, Freedom's Journal, began in 1827 because founders John Russwurm and Samuel Cornish were tired of African American stereotypes in the white press.[180] "Too long have others spoken for us," they wrote in their first issue. The African American press would go on to be a strong voice in the abolition movement and during Reconstruction, the Great Migration, both world wars and the civil rights movement. "Lynchings and riots were given considerable attention. Race progress was always applauded and Blacks were encouraged to support each other's endeavors, especially Black businesses," historian Charlotte O'Kelly writes about the content of the African American press.[181]

Ethnic media also makes ethnic and minority groups visible to civic leaders. The Tundra Times was written for Alaska's native population in the 1960s in response to the U.S. government's plans to disrupt hunting grounds. This English-language newspaper was an effort to serve the Alaskan native population, a population that speaks five languages and is spread over 400 million acres of rocky, frozen terrain. "Politicians seldom considered native or rural issues; they rarely campaigned in bush Alaska," writes historian Elizabeth James. "After Tundra Times began publishing, however, native voices became unmistakable and impossible to disregard."[182]

While ethnic media serves target audiences, they also serve the community at large. A study published in the Journal of Ethnic and Migration Studies suggested ethnic media presents points of view and stories readers won't find in the mainstream press, enriching cross-cultural understanding and creating a "multi-ethnic public sphere."[183] To that end a number of Hispanic newspapers in the U.S. are bilingual: Spanish/English, Spanish/French, Spanish/Italian, and even a trilingual newspaper, Tampa's La Gaceta, still published today,[184] in English, Spanish and Italian.[185]

"We serve as a bridge of communication between the community at large and the Latino community," says La Noticia's Hilda Gurdian. That's why she publishes editorials in English, while most other news content is in Spanish. Publishing in English may prove to be a way to keep audiences. In 2016, the Pew Research Center found that 83 percent of Hispanics said they got at least some of their news in English on a typical day.[186]

As minority populations grow, so do the chances for a more-sustained success for ethnic media. That potential, however, may lie more within the digital landscape than with traditional newspapers, television or radio. In 2016, 74 percent of Hispanics said they used the internet as a news source on a typical weekday, up from 37 percent in 2006, according to the Pew Research Center. As it is across the industry, this change has been largely influenced by millennials, who make up more than a quarter of U.S. Hispanic adults. These younger people "just don't read newspapers, but we can get them to read articles on their phone and other digital sources," says The Charlotte Post's Gerald Johnson.

One asset for many ethnic media properties is that "we have such a trusted relationship with the audience," says Hiram Jackson.[187] For one thing, Blacks and Hispanics place more importance on the media's watchdog role than non-Hispanic whites, according to the Pew Research Center. Among Blacks and Hispanics, 72 percent say news organizations' eye on political leaders helps keep them from doing what they shouldn't. [188]

Though social media and mobile news apps are increasingly the sources of news for younger readers, that trust does not always come with it. Social media can often be a free-for-all of unvetted news or fake news. "People more and more, I think, are going to rely on trusted messengers," says Sandy Close.

While Close sees ethnic media outlets in dire straits as they struggle for profits, she is also impressed by their resilience and dedication.

"The remarkable thing about ethnic media is that they survive despite being left out of most social market advertising," she says. At the same time, "The dedication of the people who persist to serve their communities is remarkable and inspiring, frankly."

Jackson is also optimistic about the future for ethnic media. "The demand for information is through the roof, especially in the Black community," he said in a September 2019 interview with the Medill News Leaders Project. "I really believe the African American community is at the forefront of re-creating who we are as a country." The problem is, "How do you monetize that? That's the challenge, and that's what we're trying to figure out."

EMBLEMS OF CHANGE IN A SOUTHERN CITY

A quarter of the largest metro areas in the country are now majority-minority cities, with a greater percentage of ethnic and minority populations than non-Hispanic white residents. Charlotte, with 873,000 residents, is the largest city in North Carolina and one of the largest in the South. It is also a majority-minority city, home to the state's largest population of African Americans and Latinos. While the number of white Charlotte residents fell to 42 percent from 65 percent over the past three decades, the Hispanic population has jumped from 1 percent in 1990 to 14 percent today. African Americans make up about a third of the population, up slightly during the same period. These demographic changes present new challenges and opportunities for Charlotte's ethnic media – eight newspapers and two digital outlets – that speak for and to communities often underserved, overlooked or left behind by traditional media. UNC Research Assistant Jeremiah Murphy explores how three publishers approach their mission and their role in shaping discussion of the important issues affecting their community.

The Charlotte Post

Charlotte Post publisher Gerald Johnson was initially reluctant to get involved with the newspaper his father, Bill, bought in 1974. But in 1986, Bill Johnson was fighting acute leukemia and asked Gerald, who already had a career developing software, to take over the business. Not fully understanding the severity of his father's condition, Gerald initially resisted. But Bill insisted, and today Gerald runs the weekly newspaper with his brother Robert, working to sustain a publication that was a prime news source for African Americans in Charlotte in the era of segregation, civil rights and the school busing controversy in the city that made national headlines in the 1970s.

Thirty-four years later, the Post is still providing local news for Charlotte and the five-county surrounding area. Its readers are older, median age 47, and with an average household income of $94,000 a year. Half have a college degree or higher. Gerald Johnson says the Post's print circulation of 15,000 today is at about half what it was at its peak in the late 1970s and early 1980s. The online edition has slightly more than 7,000 subscribers, who pay $20 a year for access. Where once the Post employed 38 people in the newsroom, it's now half that size at 19, Johnson says. But that's not surprising. By comparison, The Charlotte Observer, the largest newspaper in the state, had more than 250 in its newsroom at its peak in the 1990s, but is now down to fewer than 50.

The Charlotte Post has been a mainstay in the Black community since the latter part of the 19th century and is dealing with the same problems facing other newspapers – changing reader habits and the loss of print advertising. A survey years ago showed that African Americans considered the Post as "the most trusted and reliable source" for them in the market, Johnson says. "But now I can't say that," because it's harder to find African American readers. "We knew the zip codes that they were in," he says. "Today that's impossible to do, because African Americans are everywhere in the city now, so it's just more difficult to locate them." And younger readers aren't wedded to the print edition. The Post's website has about 45,000 unique visitors a month, and many of the paper's articles appear first online before they appear in the print newspaper, which is distributed every Thursday. "It got us a lot more eyeballs than we could ever reach with print," Johnson says.

But the trend toward digital presents the same problem for The Charlotte Post as for other newspapers. Ninety percent of revenue still comes from print and just 10 percent from digital and other sources, he says. Circulation also fell after the 2008 recession, causing advertisers to pull back across the board, especially automobile, tobacco and alcohol advertisers. "Automotive is beginning to come back," he says, but his current advertising is primarily from the financial and health care industries. Health care ads are now 20 percent of the Post's total ad revenue, and automotive represents 12 percent.

While most revenue still comes from print, production of the print paper is also the biggest expense. To boost revenue, the Post has increased prices, raising the single-copy price by 50 percent, to $1.50, and the subscription price by a similar amount, to $65 a year, including the e-edition. "It's doing well, doing a lot better than I thought it would," Johnson says. The Post is also experimenting with the ways to earn revenue with its digital edition, social media, podcasts and articles sold through Apple News. As for print, the Post will continue it for now, but "ultimately, it will disappear," Johnson says. "If we plan on being here any longer, we're going to have to change."

Qcitymetro.com

Glenn Burkins was a deputy managing editor at The Charlotte Observer in 2008 when he began noticing a number of sites springing up around the country offering hyperlocal news pitched toward specific neighborhoods and populations. "But I didn't see any serving the African American community," he says. "I was concerned the African American community would be left behind in this trend."

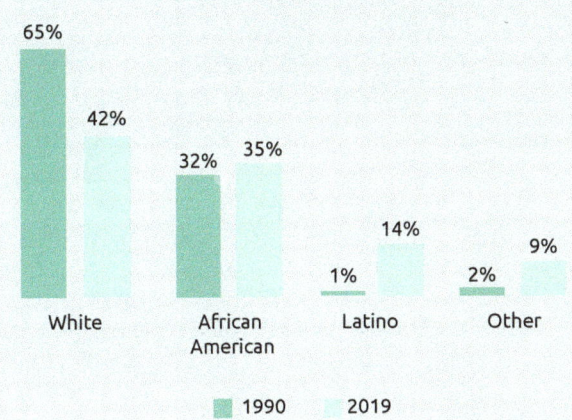

CHANGES IN DEMOGRAPHICS

■ 1990　■ 2019

Charlotte, NC has become a majority-minority city, with the largest population of African-Americans and Latinos in the state. Over the past 30 years, the percentage of white residents fell from 65 to 42 percent, while African-American and Latino communities grew.

Source: UNC Database and U.S. Census Bureau

Curious whether Charlotte could sustain a hyperlocal news site aimed at a Black audience, Burkins, at age 47, left his job at the Observer and, using personal savings, started Qcitymetro. (The Q stands for Queen, because Charlotte considers itself the Queen City.) "Call it a midlife crisis if you will," he says of his decision. Twelve years later, the web-only outlet features daily stories, social media content and "Morning Brew," a daily e-mail.

Burkins brings 34 years in the newspaper industry to the job, including work at The Wall Street Journal and the Los Angeles Times. He is a former international and White House correspondent for Knight Ridder newspapers and The Philadelphia Inquirer, and was at The Charlotte Observer for 14 years. While The Charlotte Post pays attention to hard news and appeals more to an older audience, "we are more event-oriented," Burkins says. "We aim for a younger audience than the Post." Qcitymetro has about 75,000 unique visitors a month, Burkins says, with half of Qcitymetro's audience under 40 years of age. Slightly more than a third have college degrees and make more than $80,000 annually.

Qcitymetro doesn't require a subscription to access the content on the website. Instead, Burkins asks people to buy memberships, which range from $5 a month to $80 for two years. Members receive priority tickets for events, such as an author lecture, or entry into a drawing for a traveling Broadway show. "We don't do the T-shirts and mug things. We're much more into offering them experiences," he says.

Burkins says that Qcitymetro's direct engagement with the community is crucial to maintaining readership. "We're not just some organization inside a computer. We show up at community events. We're there," he says. Qcitymetro has received a $125,000 grant from the Knight Foundation as part of an effort to expand media coverage in Charlotte's West End neighborhood, which was formerly a mostly African American community that is gentrifying. While this project has been delayed because of the coronavirus pandemic, Burkins says it might spur him to add a neighborhood print publication.

Other income comes from display ads, sponsored content and job postings. Qcitymetro's two main expenses are technology and staff – two full-time employees and roughly 10 freelancers. Burkins says "about 70 percent of our readers come from mobile devices. Whether it's Candy Crush or Solitaire or CNN or Facebook or Charlotte Observer, we're competing for screen time."

Burkins would like to add more hard news to his pages, "but hard news reporters cost money." Nevertheless, he believes "Black media is moving in the right direction," as more hyperlocal news sites serving African Americans are being established throughout the country.

"There are always unforeseen expenses. We're making money; we're paying our bills," he says, "We're better off from where we were 10 years ago, but we're still not where we want to be." But he adds, "No one has figured out this business model — Black, white or otherwise."

La Noticia

Hilda Gurdian started La Noticia in 1997, shortly after moving to Charlotte from Venezuela. The city was in the middle of a construction boom, which had attracted a growing population of Latino residents looking for work. She decided these new arrivals needed a news source geared to them.

Today, La Noticia has four city publications, with 73,000 print copies distributed free on Wednesdays in Raleigh, Asheville, and Greensboro, as well as Charlotte. It is also available free online. More than half of the readers of the print paper have attended or graduated from college, are 35 to 54 years old, and have annual incomes of $25,000 to $75,000, according to the newspaper's media kit.

Readers come from several different countries with different customs and language variations. La Noticia tries to bring these cultures together by using a standard form of Spanish and avoiding idioms peculiar to one country. "It doesn't matter where you come from, you have the same issues," she says. "If you are low income and you cannot pay your rent, it doesn't matter if you are from Puerto Rico or Mexico or Colombia."

La Noticia's focus is hyperlocal, aimed at giving people information they don't get anywhere else. The audience includes people who have been in the country for years, as well as new arrivals. "We constantly have new immigrants coming to Charlotte," Gurdian says. "They're new in the community [and] have no idea how things work here. So we continue to write [about] how to adapt to the new system, the new way of life, so they can be successful."

Like other newspaper publishers across the country, Gurdian feels pressure, mainly from the internet and the squeeze it has put on ad revenue. It used to be easier to sell advertising, Gurdian says, "just going into the businesses and talking about our readers, explaining how many people read the paper, their ages. Nowadays, it's difficult because our two main competitors, Google and Facebook, are doing many things for free. Also, our readers have more options now."

The print newspaper still accounts for about 80 percent of revenue. Print advertising is still La Noticia's largest source of revenue. "Eighty-five percent of our advertisers are the same people; they keep coming again year after year," Gurdian says. "Typically, they are grocery stores or professionals, such as dentists and immigration, personal injury and family lawyers." La Noticia also earns revenue by sponsoring events, such as LatinaCon, a conference of Latina women in politics and community service.

But Gurdian says that advertisers are increasingly interested in online ads, so she is expanding her web offerings, which have 300,000 page views a month. La Noticia is also developing a newsletter, focused on entertainment and local events, aimed at younger readers. In 2019, Google News Initiative's North America Innovation Challenge awarded La Noticia funding to develop an open-source platform for readers to submit family notices such as weddings, graduations and other celebrations. "We need to be alert and be constantly thinking about new sources of revenue to keep our operations going," Gurdian says.

Like Burkins and Johnson, Gurdian's main concern is how to make a profit and to keep serving her community. "If we go away, who is going to keep our audiences informed?" she says. "If they don't have the news and information they need to make important decisions, our democracy is going to be in trouble."

BUSINESS MODEL:
A Bigger Role for Public Broadcasting

For more than 50 years, the nation's network of 1,400 taxpayer-funded television and radio stations has entertained, educated and informed Americans with programs ranging from "Masterpiece Theatre" and "Sesame Street" to the PBS "NewsHour" and NPR's "Morning Edition." Using information and data compiled by UNC researchers, Bill Arthur, former Washington correspondent at Knight Ridder and editor for Bloomberg News, explores the potential for public broadcasting to step in and provide news coverage for residents living in a news desert.

In August 2017, readers of more than 200 newspapers in Minnesota and North Dakota found themselves looking at blank front pages: no print, no photographs. Nothing.[189] It was an effort by the Minnesota Newspaper Association to highlight newspapers' vital role in building an informed citizenry, especially in an era when so many publications are cutting staff or going out of business entirely. The intentionally blank front pages raised a key question: What would replace local newspapers if they went away?

One alternative could be public broadcasting, with its proven record in the news business through mainstays like National Public Radio (NPR), American Public Media (APM) and the Public Broadcasting Service (PBS). "Public media stations are locally controlled and operated, so they are in the best position to address growing news deserts," Kathy Merritt, senior vice president of journalism and radio at the Corporation for Public Broadcasting (CPB), told the PBS public editor in a March 2020 interview.[190]

Julie Drizin, executive director of Current,[191] a nonprofit news service covering U.S. public media, says public broadcasting is "making a difference." But, "Can public broadcasting fill the void left by the shrinking or the disappearance of newspapers? The answer is no, it can't. But it's doing the best that it can."[192]

How and whether to build on the progress that public broadcasting has made are the options confronting both policymakers and American taxpayers in the years ahead. As the two comments suggest, public broadcasting is currently well positioned to provide local and state news coverage. Its stations are easily accessible over the air throughout much of the country, especially in areas that lack high-speed internet access. Because the stations are locally controlled and operated, the stations have the flexibility to meet the unique information needs of the communities where they are located. Yet the stations are constrained by a number of factors, including available funding and staffing, as well as decades-old federal mandates to entertain and educate, as well as inform.

In an effort to understand how and where public broadcasting might step in and provide local news coverage, UNC researchers collected data on more than 1,400 outlets, including some 1,100 radio stations and 350 television stations. The research focused specifically on identifying the public broadcasting stations that provided either national or locally produced news programming. Based on an assessment of the material on their websites, about half of those outlets – 605 – were producing original content, including news shows that focused on either state or local news. This included 406 NPR stations,

144 affiliated with PBS, five with Pacifica, and 50 affiliated with APM or jointly affiliated with APM and NPR.

Widely Available, Easily Accessible

NPR is a key radio news source for many Americans, typically reaching more than 37 million people every week, with national news programs such as "Morning Edition" and "All Things Considered."[193] Americans have long rated PBS and its member stations among the most trusted institutions in the country, ranking above the court system, as well as commercial broadcasting outlets and newspapers.[194] Widely popular PBS news programs include "Frontline" and "NewsHour."

More than 95 percent of Americans can get public broadcasting's over-the-air signals, according to the Corporation for Public Broadcasting.[195] "There is no other system that covers the country like public media, evenly, fairly," says Kerri Hoffman, chief executive officer of public broadcasting's PRX, which provides programming for 200 public radio stations, including "This American Life."[196]

The Public Broadcasting Act of 1967 is the basis for the federal funding structure that exists today to support public broadcasting outlets – "valuable local community resources" that "address national concerns and solve local problems."[197] The journalism that has evolved through these outlets serves as an antidote to information overload brought on by the rise of the internet. "The internet gives people access to information, but it's a sea of information," while public broadcasting "is a curated experience," Hoffman says.[198]

The Federal Communications Commission's[199] "carve-out" of the left side of the FM radio dial years ago also created a special place for public radio, making it easily accessible for listeners. "You kind of know where to look for public radio," says Hoffman.[200] Many long-haul truckers listen to NPR because they can pick it up as they drive from state to state, says Finn Murphy, a trucker who wrote a book about his travels.[201]

While commercial television produces many high-quality news shows, commercial radio largely eschews news for music and entertainment. "Public media's near monopoly on quality … is partly a function of economics," wrote Adam Ragusea, then journalist-in-residence at Mercer University, in a 2017 paper. "There simply isn't that much money in radio anymore, so the only broadcasters that can still afford quality are [public broadcasting stations], which generally have lower fixed costs and more diverse income streams than their commercial counterparts."[202]

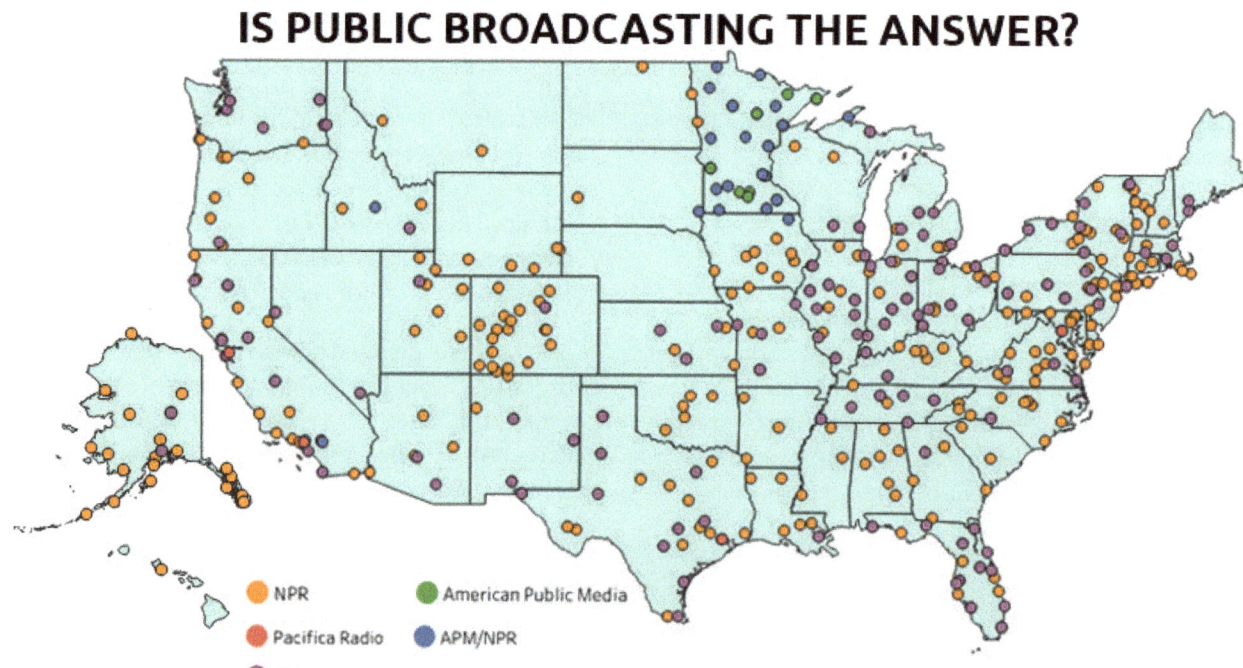

IS PUBLIC BROADCASTING THE ANSWER?

- NPR
- Pacifica Radio
- PBS
- American Public Media
- APM/NPR

About half of the 1,400 public broadcasting stations produce original content.

Source: UNC Hussman School of Journalism and Media

Paying for the Programs on Public Broadcasting

The public broadcasting system is led by the Corporation for Public Broadcasting,[203] a taxpayer-funded nonprofit organization that provides funding for public radio and television stations, but doesn't own any of the stations and doesn't produce programs. NPR and PBS are membership organizations, composed of separately licensed and operated public radio and TV stations, many owned by universities. Individual stations affiliated with NPR, APM and PBS get funding from CPB. Those stations then pay NPR and PBS membership dues and programming fees.

CPB distributed just over $400 million to public radio and television stations in fiscal 2019 out of its $445 million operating budget, mostly in the form of Community Service Grants.[204] To qualify for grants, stations must be locally owned, achieve a specified level of local financial support and provide programming that meets their community's needs and interests.[205] The formula gives extra credit for minority-owned stations. But most money for public broadcasters comes from other sources. In fiscal 2017, listener donations accounted for 38 percent of NPR's revenue, and CPB appropriations accounted for only 8 percent. The rest came from corporate donations, universities, investments, foundations and state and local governments.[206]

Overall, the U.S. "is a global outlier among democracies for how little it spends on public media," writes Victor Pickard, associate professor at the University of Pennsylvania's Annenberg School for Communication, in the Harvard Business Review. "The U.S. federal government allocates around $1.35 per person per year for public broadcasting, while Japan spends over $40 per citizen, the UK about $100, and Norway over $176."[207]

CPB grants are especially important for rural stations. Their donor base is smaller and often poorer than for urban stations. CPB grants represent 19 percent of an average rural station's revenue, with the corporation providing at least 25 percent of revenue for 113 rural stations. Thirty stations, many on Native American reservations, get at least 50 percent of their revenue from CPB.[208]

State funding is also an option for some public broadcasters, but not everywhere. Fourteen states provide no funding for public broadcasters, while 27 provide funding at less than $2 per resident. Six states fund at $2 to $4 a person, while three – South Dakota, Nebraska and Utah – fund public broadcasting at more than $4 a person. Utah is the leader, funding at $8.70 a person.[209]

There are 1,336 public radio stations and 350 public TV stations in the UNC database. About 1,000 stations are affiliated with NPR, and more than 300 television stations are affiliated with PBS. APM owns some 50 public radio stations and has an affiliation with an equal number of stations. Through its major subsidiaries – Minnesota Public Radio and Southern California Public Radio – APM produces and acquires programming from the BBC World Service and produces programming of local interest.[210] Pacifica Network owns five radio stations – in New York, Washington, Houston, Los Angeles and San Francisco – that produce original content, including podcasts, and has 200 affiliates. Mostly listener funded, it does not get CPB funding or accept corporate contributions, and is financially struggling.[211]

The Limits on Covering the News

While each state has multiple public broadcasting stations, many simply transmit programming produced by other stations. While 69 percent of NPR stations report that they offer local news, many of these stations don't produce original reporting, but merely gather and read news reported by other outlets, according to Robert Papper, who is director of an annual survey of broadcast newsrooms conducted by the Radio Television Digital News Association (RTDNA).[212]

Public television stations are even less likely than radio stations to produce local and state news programs. Only 13 PBS affiliate stations offer a daily local news broadcast, and most are in large cities, according to Papper. Maintaining a local television news staff is expensive, and local news shows do not typically have wide audience appeal. Therefore, the production costs cannot be recouped through syndication. "Doing production, even a small production at a public television station, requires space. It requires lighting and technical equipment and people," says Lynda Clarke, vice president, content grants management, at CPB.[213] Additionally, public radio and public television operate differently, says PRX's Hoffman.

> *"The hubs are unlikely to replace the granular local community reporting that is being lost as small-town newspapers fold, but on the bigger local stories, they seemingly have great potential to fill holes."*

"Public television is programmed nationally. 'Downton Abbey' is on at the same time across the whole nation," she says. "Since most things are centrally programmed, the muscles to make local content aren't there."[214]

Radio stations have more flexible programming. However, staffing of local news operations is constrained by funding. Between 2011 and 2018, more than 400 NPR stations or those that carry some NPR programming added about 1,000 full-time and part-time jobs, bringing the total to about 3,000 journalists.[215] But this hardly compensates for the 36,000 newspaper journalists lost between 2008 and 2018, according to the Bureau of Labor Statistics. So, NPR is trying to use reporters and editors more efficiently by creating regional hubs, such as the one formed in 2019 that pooled coverage among journalists in the Dallas, Houston, San Antonio and Austin stations.[216] Public radio and television journalists in Colorado, Idaho, Utah and Wyoming have formed a Mountain West News Bureau,[217] and in Kansas four stations formed a statewide news service focusing on agriculture, education, state politics, health and natural resources.

In February 2020, stations in Alabama, Louisiana and Mississippi formed a Gulf Coast hub, led by WBHM in Birmingham, Alabama. Funded with a $1.3 million grant from CPB, the hub plans to hire additional reporters and editors to boost regional coverage.[218] "Our region, sadly, has been dubbed a 'news desert.' The Gulf States need more journalism, and this collaborative effort gives us much-needed resources and the means to coordinate and leverage our coverage," said Chuck Holmes, executive director and general manager of WBHM.[219] "Does it completely fix the problem? No, it doesn't." Veterans of the Birmingham News tell him that until recently, the

paper had 70 more reporters and editors than it has now. "No way in hell I'm going to be able to raise enough money to hire 70 people," he said. But the arrangement "gives us resources we haven't had."[220]

"The hubs are unlikely to replace the granular local community reporting that is being lost as small-town newspapers fold, but on the bigger local stories, they seemingly have great potential to fill holes that are now becoming vast news deserts in much of the country," wrote Elizabeth Jensen, then NPR's public editor in a March 2020 article on the NPR website.[221]

But if public broadcasters can't replace the journalism lost when newspapers are closed, they do highlight the importance of merging legacy and online content. On their websites, public stations offer podcasts and multimedia content that never appeared on the air. "All media are now merging," says Howard Husock, a former board member of the CPB. "Radio is video, video is audio, and they can be print, too."[222]

"You're seeing more collaboration between public broadcasters and other media," and even some acquisitions, says Julie Drizin of Current. Several public radio stations have bought digital sites in their respective cities that offer local news and entertainment information. For example, WAMU[223] in Washington acquired DCist, WNYC in New York bought the Gothamist, KPCC in Los Angeles acquired LAist, and Colorado Public Radio acquired the Denverite.[224]

"The future is around digital," says PRX's Hoffman. To her, the discussion shouldn't just be about splitting resources between radio and television but "thinking about nonprofit news operations as partners in a broader ecosystem."[225] That's one reason the Radio-Television News Directors Association changed its name a few years ago to the Radio Television Digital News Association[226] and why some media experts, such as Steve Coll, dean of the Columbia University Graduate School of Journalism, have suggested that the CPB be renamed the Corporation for Public Media.[227]

A Path to the Future

As concerned Americans sought information about the coronavirus pandemic in early 2020, audience figures for NPR rose sharply, with 67 million unique visitors to npr.org in early 2020, surpassing the previous high of 58 million in November 2016 during the election.[228] However, the economic fallout from the coronavirus has also caused many corporate underwriters to curb their contributions, and listeners who suddenly lost their jobs are unlikely to be enthusiastic donors. Some of the stations that had planned fund drives in March 2020 held off. "How do you fundraise in the middle of a pandemic?" asks Mike Wall, general manager at KMXT-FM in Kodiak, Alaska. "I don't want to be the guy going on the air in the middle of the virus saying, 'Hey, by the way, now give us some dough.'"[229]

This leaves many public stations more reliant on federal funding. Calls to eliminate federal funding for public broadcasting go almost as far back as the Public Broadcasting Act. More recently, Republican presidential candidate Mitt Romney declared in 2012: "I'm going to stop the subsidy to PBS." When Congress included $75 million for CPB in its coronavirus emergency stimulus measure in March 2020, Republican Rep. Jim Jordan of Ohio said the bill should focus on fighting the virus, not supporting "liberal projects."[230] The Trump administration has consistently proposed to defund CPB, but Congress has ignored the idea, appropriating $445 million annually for the ninth straight year in fiscal 2020. [231]

"I think one of the most brilliant things that was ever done at CPB was to give the money to the stations instead of NPR and PBS," says Laura Walker, former president and chief executive officer at WNYC[232]. "It's brilliant because every single senator and Congress person has a local station in their market, and they know how much people

rely on those stations because they appear on those stations," which are often one of the few outlets for a politician to gain recognition.[233]

Former CBP board member Howard Husock thinks it's important "to repurpose the funding rather than reduce the funding." Stations spend large chunks of the CPB grant money paying dues to NPR and PBS and fees for programs such as NPR's "Morning Edition" and "All Things Considered." As a result, the stations end up retaining very little of the federal funds, and, "in effect, the money is recycled to Washington," he says. Calling the 1967 broadcasting act "superannuated," Husock suggests changing the formula to let stations keep more of the money for local programming and to get more money to small stations in lower-income regions. "You're not spending it as wisely as you might if your goal is to encourage local journalism," he says.[234]

But is more needed? What should be the role of public television, which has largely been focused on national news? Is there more that could be done by public television stations in providing statewide news? How is current and future funding best allocated between PBS and NPR? With more funding, what else could NPR stations be doing to reverse the loss of news at the state and regional level?

It is "clear that the market cannot provide for all of our communication and information needs," wrote University of Pennsylvania professor Victor Pickard. "We must expand on and repurpose America's public broadcasting system to serve as a core democratic infrastructure, one that provides news and information, as well as cultural and educational fare, to everyone across all platforms and media types."[235]

The coronavirus crisis may provide an opportunity "to restructure public media to better address the needs of our public," PRX's Hoffman wrote in Medium, an online publishing platform. This could include greater collaboration among PBS, NPR and APM. "The public media system we have today in many ways reflects past realities better than current demands;" she wrote. "It's almost become cliché to say that if we could start from scratch, it would look different."[236]

TECHNOLOGICAL CAPABILITIES:
The Algorithm as Editor

What happens when an algorithm selects your news? In 2018, Facebook released a mobile product, called "Today In," which uses an algorithm to select articles from various news outlets and then provides Facebook users with a daily feed of local news and information. As of May 2020, "Today In" was available in more than 6,000 communities. Using proprietary data provided by Facebook in 2019, as well as more recent samplings, researchers at the UNC Hussman School of Journalism and Media examined the timeliness, relevance and type of local news stories available in North Carolina communities.

Hurricane Dorian made landfall on the Outer Banks of North Carolina on Sept. 5, 2019, causing flooding and trapping hundreds of people on Ocracoke Island. Almost 200 miles inland in the university community of Chapel Hill, subscribers to Facebook's "Today In Chapel Hill" found two stories about the hurricane in their daily local news feed. One was a day-old story from a local radio station: "Chapel Hill Preparing Ahead of Impact from Hurricane Dorian, Future Hurricanes," which had also been featured the previous day, Sept. 4. The second, from a Fox-affiliated television station in Greensboro, 50 miles to the west of Chapel Hill, was three days old, "Raleigh-Durham Airport monitoring Hurricane Dorian for potential impact." There was no news on the progress of the hurricane.

During the first week of April 2020 – a week after the governor of North Carolina had issued a stay-at-home order – "Today In Chapel Hill" featured several stories related to the coronavirus pandemic. Those stories included useful information about what to do if sheltering in place with a domestic abuser, suspension of weekly yard waste pick-up, and a request for food donations for the county emergency operations. But there were no articles that placed into context regional trends in the greater Raleigh-Durham metro area, which

includes Chapel Hill. There were also a number of stories from outside the Chapel Hill community – about the International Space Station, a foal found on the Outer Banks, the arrest of boxing promoter Floyd Mayweather's daughter in Houston, and a story datelined Conroe, Texas, about a woodcarver making canes for veterans.

Facebook launched "Today In" in 2018, based on research that found users of the social media platform wanted more local news.[237] The free mobile product, available only on smartphones and tablets, draws content from more than 1,200 news publishers every week. In May 2020, it was available in some 6,000 towns and cities[238] – including more than 225 North Carolina communities – and, according to Facebook, 1.6 million people used the feature, which typically posts five top stories a day. The news feed also includes announcements from local governments and school systems.

Facebook does not produce the news on "Today In." Instead, the algorithm that powers the mobile product selects from content that is produced mostly by newspapers and television and radio stations. If publishers want their articles posted on "Today In," they must register so Facebook can identify them as legitimate news operations. But with the demise of more than 2,100 local newspapers over the past 15 years, there is a dearth of local news in many communities. For a town that has lost its local newspaper, such as Chapel Hill, the algorithm that selects the news often produces quirky results. Users can feel as if they are in a time warp (as was the case with Hurricane Dorian), or scratch their heads as to why feature stories with out-of-state datelines are considered local news. Even in major metro areas such as Raleigh-Durham, where there are multiple news outlets, including regional television stations and newspapers, the algorithm can still fail to pick up on major news stories and prize-winning investigative series produced by those outlets. "It's still a work in progress," says Josh Mabry, Facebook's local news partnerships lead.[239]

More Americans get news on social media sites than from print newspapers, and Facebook is the dominant social media site for news, with about 43 percent of Americans getting their news from there.[240] "Today In" is one of several major efforts by Facebook to address the rise of news deserts, including a pledge in 2019 to spend more than $300 million over three years to foster partnerships with local news organizations.[241] In 2019, the social media company also launched "Facebook News," which highlights the top national stories of the day selected both by an algorithm and a team of editors and curators employed by Facebook.[242]

The University of North Carolina is one of four universities provided proprietary data from Facebook in 2019, consisting of 314,000 links to news stories in the "Today In" news feed for the month of February. While researchers at other institutions analyzed national trends,[243] UNC researchers focused on analyzing what sort of local news was available to residents in 15 metro areas in North Carolina where "Today In" data was then available.[244] In addition, the researchers updated and supplemented their findings by sampling the "Today In" news feeds for Raleigh, Durham and Chapel Hill in September 2019 and April 2020.[245]

Facebook estimates there is not enough local news (minimum five stories a day) to launch "Today In" in about one in three communities.[246] But even in areas where there is enough news, the algorithm often shapes a news diet that is very different from what is offered by a traditional news outlet, such as a newspaper or television station. The algorithm for "Today In" selects news items posted on Facebook based on a variety of factors, which,

according to Facebook, includes the timeliness of the article and local relevance, which is, in part, a measure of how often an article is shared in a certain area.

UNC analysis found that the algorithm's reliance on the number of shares in a certain time period can determine how timely the article is when it is posted, the type of information it conveys and the source (whether it is from television stations or newspapers). Here are some of the major findings:

1. **Many of the articles** on the "Today In" news feed were two or more days old. During the last week in September 2019, for example, more than half of the stories on the "Today In" news feeds for Raleigh, Durham and Chapel Hill were two to four days old.

2. **Almost half of the stories posted** in North Carolina communities in February and September of 2019 concerned either crime or human interest. The crime stories tended to deal with on-going cases or single acts of violence. Typical human interest and crime stories included, "She thought she rescued a kitten. It turned out to be a bobcat" and "Durham police investigating after man found shot dead in parking lot."

3. **Because crime and human interest dominated,** there were far fewer big-picture stories covering such topics as education, health, politics, infrastructure, economic development or the environment – all topics that the Federal Communications Commission has identified as "critical information needs" for residents of any community.[247]

4. **There was a disconnect between** what was considered major news that appeared on the front page of newspapers and what appeared on "Today In." Almost half of the articles on local newspaper front pages during February 2019 analyzed by UNC dealt with political, education or health issues, compared with 13 percent on the "Today In" sites. (Table 1) For example, on Feb. 22, 2019, The News and Observer ran a front page story about the state election board voting to hold a special election in North Carolina's Ninth Congressional District because of election fraud in 2018, a story with major local and statewide implications. The

algorithm didn't pick up that story, but instead posted a story on "Today in Raleigh" and "Today in Greensboro" about a man in Raleigh renting a hotel room to a prostitute who was a minor. Greensboro is in a different media market than Raleigh, and 75 miles away. (See Table 2 for percent of stories from newspapers on "Today In.")

5. **In large metro areas,** with multiple media outlets, there are more stories from regional television stations than newspapers. This is likely because television stations have much larger social media followings than newspapers, and, as a result, their stories get shared more often. WRAL in Raleigh, for example, has more than 600,000 Facebook followers compared with 115,000 for The News and Observer.[248] Almost 90 percent of the stories in September posted on the news feeds for Raleigh and Durham came from the local television stations. This compares with only 50 percent in Chapel Hill.

6. **Outside the major metro areas,** most of the stories on "Today In" came from newspapers. Overall, slightly more than half of the stories came from newspapers, while a third came from television stations. But even in mid-sized markets that did not have a major regional television news operation, "Today In" tended to select feature stories, not the major news stories that made the front page of local newspapers. For example, stories in The Fayetteville Observer in February 2019 about downtown parking, officials seeking additional tax revenue and food stamp benefits were not posted, while feature stories about a church rebuilding after Hurricane Mathew and another about the Tuskegee Airmen of World War II were.

Researchers at the University of Minnesota and Duke University had similar insights when they analyzed the massive trove of proprietary data on the 400 "Today In" news feeds active in February 2019. To quickly and efficiently analyze the data, they devised their own algorithm that used headlines on the 314,000 links provided by Facebook to determine the type of story – such as sports, emergencies, obituaries, or schools. They were able to classify about half of the links (149,000) into 10 broad categories.[249] Eight of those categories (such as emergencies and public safety, education, and health) were identified as serving a "critical information need."[250]

WHEN AN ALGORITHM CHOOSES YOUR NEWS

Share of News Articles per Category by "Today In" and Newspaper Front Pages (Percentages) in 2019

Category	"Today In"	Front Pages
Emergency/Safety	26 %	14 %
Health	2	3
Education	4	10
Transport Systems	4	3
Environment	<1	2
Econ. Dev.	8	8
Civic Info.	10	5
Political Life	7	31
Sports	7	1
H./C. Interest	22	23
Obituary	6	1

Table 1

Share of Front-Page Articles on "Today In" (Percentages) in 2019

Category	Share of Articles
Fayetteville Observer	13
Gaston Gazette	16
News & Observer	5
News & Record	1
Salisbury Post	8
Winston-Salem Journal	11

Table 2

Source: UNC analysis of Facebook data

Using their own algorithm to sort the stories, the researchers concluded that 60 percent – or 89,000 stories – delivered critical information and news. However, that conclusion was heavily skewed by the number of articles about emergencies and public safety, which includes crime stories. Almost half of the stories classified as delivering critical information were in the emergencies and public safety category, and it was the second most popular category, accounting for 28 percent of total stories. Articles on other critical topics – such as education and politics – fared more poorly, with education stories accounting for only 9 percent and political stories for only 2 percent of the total. Sports stories were the most popular stories in February 2019, accounting for almost a third – more even than emergencies and crime.

Unlike the UNC researchers, the researchers at Duke and the University of Minnesota did not click through to the links to determine timeliness, source or local relevance. Also, they did not compare which major stories were featured on the front pages of local newspapers that were not picked up by "Today In."[251] However, both studies found that the most popular stories on "Today In" are those involving breaking news (emergencies and crime) or human interest and sports.

Josh Mabry, Facebook's local news partnerships lead, points out, "People can also find local news and community information in other areas of Facebook – [including] publishers they are connected to in News Feed – or products such as Local Alerts, which provides critical information to communities directly from local governments and first responders." Facebook's COVID-19 Information Center, for example, has daily updates on the progression of cases in their region, information from local authorities and a feature called Community Help that allows users to request or offer to assist neighbors, as well as donate to relief efforts.

Both research studies, however, concluded that Facebook users who relied exclusively on the "Today In" feature for local news coverage would most likely miss important local governmental, political, economic and educational stories that are written and produced by other news outlets. "Facebook [is] not covering the news," Jennifer Parker, editor and publisher of the Cross Roads News in Decatur, Georgia, told the Medill News Leaders Project in September 2019. "They're not covering local government, they're not covering our local schools."[252] Instead, Facebook is relying on an algorithm that picks news based on what engages users and prompts sharing. Assuming a journalist attends a local planning board meeting and writes a story about it – not always a certainty given the number of local newspapers that have vanished – that type of story is not typically shared as widely on social media as crime or human interest stories.

In June 2020, Facebook announced it would discontinue "Today In" as a separate product, and, instead, would make the local news feed available through Facebook News, which features national news drawn from some of the country's leading news organizations. In contrast to the "Today In" feature, Facebook News doesn't rely solely on artificial intelligence to select the articles. It also employs a team of about 30 curators to exercise editorial judgment, and choose the most important stories.[253]

"When we started talking to news organizations about building Facebook News earlier this year, they emphasized that original reporting is more expensive to produce and better recognized by seasoned journalists than by algorithms. So to help reward this kind of work, we formed a curation team [with editorial independence] to manage the "Today's Stories" section of Facebook News," Campbell Brown, Facebook vice president for global news partnerships, said in announcing the launch.[254] In addition, some major news organizations with content on Facebook News – including The New York Times, Wired and News Corp. – "are being paid for their content … so we can have access to more of their content."[255]

However, Facebook currently has no plans to supplement the selection of local news articles, formerly on "Today In" and now on Facebook News, by hiring additional curators who can identify important stories that might have been overlooked by the algorithm. Nor does Facebook plan to pay the vast majority of local news organizations for their stories, contending that the local news feed will drive users to the originating news sites. However, many of the links UNC researchers tested were behind paywalls and required users to subscribe in order to read the entire story. This most likely discourages users from remaining on the local news organizations' sites.

"As we add more local news to Facebook News, we will continue testing, updating and improving the algorithm," said Mabry. "We will continue adding more tools for people to control their news experience such as specifying their location for more local news and tying their paid subscriptions [to news outlets] to Facebook News."

"Today In" was designed to address the desires of Facebook users to see more local news on the social media platform. But Facebook is confronting two issues as it attempts to provide its users with timely and relevant local news, based on UNC analysis. First, the quantity of local news in many markets has fallen off dramatically in recent years with the closure of hundreds of local newspapers and the layoffs of thousands of local journalists. As a result, feature stories from outside the community, and even outside the state, appeared frequently on the local news feeds in North Carolina towns and cities, and half were two or more days old.

There is also a quality issue. Unlike with Facebook News, there is no editor exercising judgment about which local story is more important – a story about a special congressional election versus a story about a tawdry murder. Left to its own devices, without human intervention, the algorithm that selects local news stories is doing exactly what it was designed to do – choosing stories based on a programmed set of criteria that weighs popularity with users, as measured by the number of shares. Therefore, "When you're looking for actual, original local reporting that fills a critical information need, it's still newspapers that are, by far, the primary source," says Philip Napoli, professor of public policy at Duke University and author of an exhaustive study in 2018 that looks at the local news available in 100 mid-sized cities in the country.[256]

Researchers Bill Arthur, Justin Kavlie (Ph.D. '21), and Jeremiah Murphy (M.A. '19) compiled data and provided analysis for this article.

REGULATIONS:
The State of Play

*S*enators and congressional representatives, as well as national and state policymakers, are considering a variety of bills and policy revisions to support local news. Dana Miller Ervin, an award-winning journalist for "60 Minutes" and "Nightline" and staffer on Capitol Hill for over a decade, reviews what has been proposed and each plan's current status.

*I*f the pandemic is decimating local news, it's also prompting lawmakers to consider how to help the struggling industry. "It's as if for the first time, people on the Hill care about newspapers," says Seattle Times publisher and Capitol Hill watcher Frank Blethen.

"Before the pandemic, journalism was seen as a pet interest on the Hill," says Viktorya Vilk of the news advocacy group PEN America. "That perception has shifted now. We're finally at a moment when conversations [about assistance] are absolutely happening."

The shift is apparent both in the number of concerned lawmakers and in the breadth of their proposals. Before the pandemic, congressional efforts were narrowly tailored. None called for direct spending. Today there are several serious proposals to direct funds to local media, and hundreds of lawmakers from both parties have written to House and Senate leadership expressing their support.

"I get the sense there's more support," says seasoned lobbyist Paul Boyle, "but will that translate into meaningful relief quickly?" As of this writing, only one industry-specific stimulus measure has become law: a $75 million appropriation for public broadcasting. And much

of that will go to public television stations, which produce very little local news.

News advocacy groups are optimistic that Congress' newfound concern about expanding news deserts not only will result in short-term assistance, but also create momentum after the COVID crisis subsides, perhaps bolstering support for long-standing proposals. But that hope is tempered by the election year reality that congressional business will slow as campaigns intensify, so proposals that don't get adopted soon will wait until January.

Concern about their local papers has galvanized many Republicans to support immediate COVID-19 assistance for local outlets, but they may be less willing to support many broader longer-term measures because of opposition from their base. The Coronavirus Aid, Relief and Economic Security (CARES) Act's $75 million for public broadcasting is a case in point. It was slammed by a Tea Party leader, Rep. Jim Jordan, R-Ohio, as "a liberal pet project," and conservatives lambasted the aid on Facebook. "They don't like the media, but they care about their local paper and its coverage of them," News Media Alliance's Boyle explains.

"Before the pandemic, journalism was seen as a pet interest on the Hill. That perception has shifted now."

Given the hostility to journalists fomented by the president's "enemy of the people" trope, it's likely that any longer-term assistance be narrowly tailored, perhaps like some of the proposals discussed in this chapter.[257] Some already have bipartisan and bicameral support.

This review highlights a number of current proposals, those now in play because of the pandemic and others that are currently before Congress or have achieved some measure of success. Although this review necessarily focuses on the 116th Congress, many of the proposals are long-standing and will likely be reintroduced next year.

Direct Government Support: SBA Loans

There is so far no data on the number of newsrooms that have received stimulus loans from the Small Business Administration. The Paycheck Protection Program (PPP), a COVID response initiative, allows small businesses that need immediate capital to borrow up to eight weeks of payroll costs.[258] Recipients that maintain payroll will have their loans forgiven.

The Tampa Bay Times, The Seattle Times and the National Enquirer say they've received loans, but chain-owned newsrooms reportedly have been unable to qualify for assistance, barred because of the size of their parent companies. There is irony that consolidation, with its closures and layoffs, is now preventing emaciated newsrooms from getting relief.[259] [260]

On April 20, Sen. Maria Cantwell, D-Wash., took to the abandoned floor of the Senate to call for a waiver of SBA's "affiliation rules." The waiver would allow local newsrooms owned by larger parent companies to qualify for the PPP loans. Restaurants and hotels received a similar waiver in an earlier stimulus bill, but that carve-out turned controversial when the public learned large companies like Shake Shack and Ruth's Chris Steak House received the loans before funding ran out, so smaller businesses went without help.

Lobbying efforts by Cantwell and a bipartisan group of senators were matched by those of a similar bipartisan group of over 100 representatives in the House, and Democrats included the measure in their proposal for a coronavirus relief bill, the Health and Economic Recovery Opportunity Omnibus Emergency Solutions Act (HEROES Act).[261] [262]

Republicans say the House bill, crafted without Republican input, is dead on arrival in the Senate. Sens. Cantwell; Amy Klobuchar, D-Minn.; John Kennedy, R-La.; and John Boozman, R-Ark., continue to lobby for a waiver, but convincing Senate Leadership may be difficult because of the outcry over the restaurant waiver.

The availability of PPP loans seems to be altering a long-standing debate among journalists about the desirability of government aid. Even before the pandemic, the former dean of the Columbia Journalism School, Nicholas Lemann, argued that the local news crisis had become so severe that only direct government support could save it.[263] Many journalists opposed the idea, worrying that government funding would compromise editorial independence.

But concern the pandemic has become an extinction event has now softened, though not stilled, those voices. After some journalists argued against taking the PPP loans, Los Angeles Times correspondent Matt Pearce tweeted, "I appreciate the discussion, but if journalists don't get their oxygen masks on first, we're not gonna be around to help the people around us."[264]

Direct Government Support: Public Service Ads

News advocacy groups believe an increase in revenue from public-service ads could help some newsrooms survive the pandemic. They'd like to see the administration place more ads with local news outlets, and a lot of congressmen agree. On April 20, nearly 250 House members wrote to the president, asking him to direct more of the government's $1 billion ad budget

"If journalists don't get their oxygen masks on first, we're not gonna be around to help the people around us."

Several bills that can assist local news organizations are currently before Congress.

to local media. They also want the administration to "incentivize" expenditure of stimulus funds on local ads.[265]

There are no estimates of how much of the government's current ad budget could be redirected, and it's up to the administration to decide whether it will heed the request. Given the current administration's attitude toward journalism, that could be a tough sell. But the letter is important because it was signed by members of both the right-wing Freedom Caucus and the left-wing Progressive Caucus, underscoring broad support for local journalism.

The proposal could receive legislative support. Democratic Congressman Tim Ryan of Ohio is sponsoring a bill that would, among other things, require that 50 percent of current government advertising be placed with local news outlets.[266] [267] Ryan and eight House Democrats unsuccessfully lobbied Speaker Nancy Pelosi to include this and other proposals in the Democrats' HEROES Act.

It was only after the Democrats' stimulus bill passed the House without their inclusion that Ryan filed his local media bill, indicating he'll continue to lobby for assistance.

A number of news lobbyists want the government to go further and have asked Congress to appropriate additional money for the ads.[268] The most powerful of these, the National Association of Broadcasters and the News Media Alliance, have asked for $5–$10 billion for additional ad spending. [269]

Journalists who worry about the influence of government money have yet to voice the same objection to spending on ads. Perhaps that's because papers have always relied on government-funded postal subsidies and legal notices. But local governments have been accused of pulling ads from papers with critical coverage.[270] That's why those who argue that local news cannot survive without government support usually advocate for some form of firewall between legislators and journalists.

Legislation and Bills on Capitol Hill

There are several proposals before Congress that address the local news crisis.
Here are some of the ideas proposed.

Proposal	What It Proposes	Status
The Coronavirus Aid, Relief and Economic Security Act (CARES Act)	$3 trillion stimulus package provided $75 million for public broadcasting and allowed some employers to delay required pension payments until 2021.	Passed both House and Senate, and signed by President Trump.
Health and Economic Recovery Opportunity Omnibus Emergency Solutions Act (HEROES Act)	Allows newsrooms owned by chains to qualify for small business loans.	Passed in House along party lines. No chance of Senate passage.
Protect Local Media Act, sponsored by Tim Ryan (D-OH)	Requires executive agencies to spend half of advertising dollars with local media. Amends the PPP program so that publishers with 500 or fewer employees can receive loans. Creates a credit up to $20k for each new journalism hire. Makes it easier for commercial news outlets to transform themselves into non-profits.	No progress since May 15, 2020 filing.
The Saving Local News Act, sponsored by Rep. Mark DeSaulnier (D-CA)	Amends the Internal Revenue Code to make it easier for commercial news outlets to transform themselves into tax-exempt organizations, exempts ad revenues from taxation, and requires IRS to rule on applications within 12 months.	No progress since June 5, 2019 filing.
Journalism Competition and Preservation Act, sponsored by Rep. David Cicilline (D-RI)	Gives individual news organizations a four-year window to collectively negotiate with tech giants without violating anti-trust regulations.	Filed in 2018, but gained bipartisan support in 2019 in both House and Senate. Co-Sponsors include: Amy Klobuchar (D-MN), Rand Paul (R-KY) and Mitch McConnell (R-KY).

Source: Congress.gov

Legal Fixes: Pension Debt Relief

Unable to pay its $125 million pension bill, the 160-year-old McClatchy Co. filed for bankruptcy earlier this year. The country's second-largest newspaper chain had long struggled under the weight of its $800 million pension debt. Now the federal government will likely assume responsibility for the underfunded plan.[271]

McClatchy is not the only paper to grapple with an underfunded pension plan. Like other businesses with legacy plans created when defined benefits were common, many have found it difficult to come up with the cash to pay off pension shortfalls.

Now the COVID recession is exacerbating those problems. Stock market losses have reduced the value of plan assets, which means the shortfalls are greater. Because current low interest rates reduce plan earnings, they also push up the amount of quarterly pension contributions plan administrators must make to cover those shortfalls. The combination may be disastrous for many already-struggling news outlets with underfunded plans.

The timing is awful. Pension payments were already set to increase next year as statutory interest rate modifications begin to be phased out. The American Benefits Council, a trade association for large employers, says the cumulative effect of the COVID recession and the rule modifications is a perfect storm. It estimates that pension bills could double next year, increasing payments owed by as much as $24 billion.[272]

The stimulus bill called the CARES Act (Coronavirus Aid, Relief and Economic Security) gave employers some temporary protection from increases by delaying required payment of 2020 bills until 2021. Gannett CEO Mike Reed told investors that this will increase liquidity this year by $50 million.[273]

But the CARES Act omitted more extensive relief contained in the HEROES Act, including a provision specific to community newspapers.[274] Both business and news advocates are lobbying hard for adoption of these protections.

Business lobbyists want Congress to allow employers to calculate their payments using higher interest rates and allow payments over 15 years instead of seven.[275]

Newspaper lobbyists want a more-generous break. They want Congress to expand a provision in last year's budget that lowered pension payments for a limited number of newspapers so more can take advantage of the relief.

That measure – the brainchild of Seattle Times publisher Frank Blethen – allowed family-owned, community papers that operate in only one state to reduce quarterly payments by assuming high interest rates. It also allowed them to stretch out payments over 30 years.

It took Blethen five years to get congressional approval for his bill. "We were told you can't get special-interest legislation anymore, but we were desperate, so we just kept trying." He didn't think anyone would help large chains, so he narrowly tailored the bill.

The Congressional Budget Office said the measure would add slightly to tax revenues, since papers would have more taxable income.[276] But some conservatives opposed the measure, arguing that papers are more likely to go belly up during the longer payback window, so their pension debt would be assumed by the taxpayer.[277]

The provision ultimately succeeded because Blethen enlisted the support of both Democratic and Republican members of Washington state's congressional delegation and encouraged other community papers to lobby their members. "It helped that Chuck Schumer realized he had two to three family-owned papers in New York," Blethen says, and he "tweaked" the bill to include them. McClatchy papers lobbied to be included. "We heard they were in, but then they weren't," Blethen says. "No one knows what happened."

Newspaper lobbyists succeeded in getting the expansion of Blethen's bill in the Democrats' HEROES Act, but the measure will likely have a tougher time in the Senate, where its opponents have worked hard to prevent its passage.

Blethen estimates that his provision in the 2020 budget will help 20 papers. The newspaper trade association, the News Media Alliance, says the HEROES Act expansion will help at least another five or six chains or publishers, including McClatchy.[278] McClatchy is mum on whether revised pension rules can still help the bankrupt chain, with the sale slated for July.

Ironically, the McClatchy bankruptcy may help persuade some lawmakers to give more papers pension relief. The federal agency responsible for bailing out pension plans – the Pension Benefit Guaranty Corporation – announced it may inherit McClatchy's pension plan.[279] That's a costly result that might have been forestalled had Congress approved pension relief last December.

Indirect Government Support: Tax Credits for Newsroom Employment

In posts that read like obituaries, a Poynter Institute list of newsroom layoffs, furloughs and closures details the toll of the COVID recession.[280] The loss of those jobs is a deepening crisis. Newspapers lost half their newsroom employees between 2008 and 2019, leaving behind many emaciated newsrooms unable to adequately cover their communities.[281]

Journalist groups are pressing for a variety of measures to slow the newest round of cuts. The NewsGuild labor union and the advocacy group PEN America have both written to congressional leadership asking for emergency funding to prevent more layoffs. Another advocacy group, Free Press, is lobbying both for direct financial support and for tax credits aimed at maintaining and growing newsroom staff.[282]

So far Tim Ryan's Protect Local Media Act is the only congressional measure to contain a news-specific employment tax credit.[283] It would create a credit of up to $20,000 for each new journalism hire.

Ryan unsuccessfully urged Pelosi to include this in the HEROES Act. However, the Democrats' bill includes two broader job support programs that could benefit some journalists.

The bill would expand the Employee Retention Credit, introduced in an earlier stimulus measure.[284] It would allow struggling businesses to reduce their employment tax bills by up to $36,000 per employee.

The HEROES fund also creates a $13/hour bonus for "essential workers" who continued to report to work and could not telework. Essential work includes news gathering and dissemination.

The News Media Alliance, which says it supports both measures, believes there is some Republican support for expansion of the Employee Retention Credit. So far, Mitt Romney of Utah is the only Republican senator to support bonus pay for essential workers.[285] His Patriot Pay proposal creates a 75 percent refundable payroll tax credit for a bonus of up to $12 an hour for essential workers in critical industries. Congress and the Department of Labor would designate those industries deemed to be critical.

Legal Fixes: Helping Newsrooms Become Nonprofits

The Great Recession, responsible for the demise of hundreds of papers, also inspired journalists to create nonprofit newsrooms, more reliant on donations than ad revenue. The Institute for Nonprofit News last year reported that new sites have launched at the rate of one a month for 12 years. Some, like ProPublica, produce national news, but half of the institute's 240 members are state or local news sites.

Nonprofits seem better prepared to survive the COVID recession than do for-profit outlets. The institute's director, Sue Cross, says donations to many organizations increased during the first months of the pandemic as interest in news drove traffic to their sites. Revenue from live events declined, however, and Cross worries that a protracted downturn will hurt foundation endowments, thus limiting available grant funding.

Some journalists want Congress to make it easier for commercial news outlets to transform themselves into tax-exempt organizations.[286] Rep. Mark DeSaulnier, D-Calif., has sponsored a bill to ease the conversion, and Rep. Tim Ryan, D-Ohio, recently filed a similar proposal.[287]

DeSaulnier's bill, the Saving Local News Act, amends the Internal Revenue Code to clarify that entities which are organized and operated exclusively for publishing written news articles can qualify to become tax-exempt organizations. The bill also exempts any ad revenues from taxation and requires the IRS to rule on news applications within 12 months.

The bill has made little progress since it was filed a year ago, and some news advocates question whether there's a significant constituency for the bill. Sue Cross says her members have had little difficulty winning tax-exempt status. Last fall, the first large commercial paper to become a nonprofit, The Salt Lake Tribune, found the transformation surprisingly easy.

The Tribune successfully argued to the IRS that it qualified to be a nonprofit organization under current law because it is owned and operated exclusively for educational and charitable activities, both of which are already listed as tax-exempt purposes. The IRS signed off on the application in only five months.[288]

But IRS actions may not always be so quick or favorable. In approving tax-exempt status for The Tribune, former Columbia Law School Dean David Schizer says, the IRS moved away from past rulings that denied the applications of news outlets. A 1977 IRS ruling that is still on the books could be invoked to again make the conversion difficult.[289] If the IRS returns to this approach, DeSaulnier's clarifying amendment could be helpful.[290]

It is worth noting that nonprofit newsrooms, like all tax-exempt organizations, cannot endorse political candidates. The Salt Lake Tribune says it was willing to trade endorsements for an additional source of revenue. It points out it can continue to publish editorials on actions by officeholders. But others may be hesitant to forgo this important community service, which is especially important as voters make decisions about local races, many of which receive less coverage.

Direct Government Support: Corporation for Public Broadcasting

The Corporation for Public Broadcasting received an appropriation of $445 million in the fiscal year 2020, but most of the support for the nation's 1,500 public broadcasting stations comes from donations and corporate sponsorships, which reportedly have declined because of the pandemic. CPB received $75 million to help small and rural stations compensate for the losses, but that amount won't make up for the lost income, and news advocates think CPB could receive an additional supplement.[291]

Some journalists see CPB as a model for the distribution of government aid because it successfully functions as a political firewall between funders and stations.[292] They think the agency should be tasked with distributing emergency pandemic assistance to news organizations outside the public broadcasting system.

Free Press believes Congress should create an emergency fund for local news jobs and that CPB should distribute money to both nonprofit and for-profit newsrooms.[293] Steve Waldman of Report for America argues that CPB should help fund all nonprofit news outlets, not just public broadcasters.[294] He'd also like Congress to rewrite the statutory formula that governs most of the corporation's funding decisions, directing more money to public radio stations trying to improve local news.

But many journalists think CPB should be revamped altogether to address the crisis in local news. They argue that corporation's original mission is outdated. Americans today no longer need an alternative to the "vast wasteland" of commercial television.[295] [296] Television is in a "Golden Age" in which audiences can stream award-winning entertainment from around the globe. Audiences need news about their communities, they argue, not reruns of "Downton Abbey."

Former CPB board member and self-described conservative Howard Husock is the most prolific advocate of this refocusing. He points out that public television – which receives about three-quarters of CPB's appropriation – produces almost no local news, while many public radio newsrooms are underfunded.[297]

Husock's argument is supported by data from a survey conducted jointly by the Radio Television Digital News Association and Hofstra University. It shows only 13 of the country's 169 public television stations run a daily local newscast.[298] Two-thirds of public radio stations broadcast local news, but the survey's author, Robert Papper, says budgets are so tight that many struggle to support just a single reporter.[299]

Husock's proposal, which he's pitched to House and Senate commerce committees, would rewrite CPB's statutory funding model.[300] It would eliminate the requirement that radio stations spend a large percentage of their grant on national programming. He believes that NPR could be self-sufficient, although the national syndicator has announced it may cut staff positions because of the pandemic. Husock would also end the requirement that funds be used for the infrastructure of television distribution. He says these and other changes would allow stations to expand their investments in local journalism without increasing CPB's annual appropriation.

Whatever the merits or deficits of Husock's idea, it has never been translated into bill language, and there is no visible support for amendment of CPB's authorizing legislation. And amending the statute is perilous at the current time when journalism-bashing is a popular political tactic.

But some point out that CPB can receive additional funding without an amendment of the law. The corporation received an additional $20 million for infrastructure in its FY 2020 budget as well as the $75 million stimulus supplement. They argue that Congress should give CPB additional funding for local news, which can then be used by station managers as they see fit.

Market–Based Relief: Increasing Advertising Revenues From Digital Sites

More than half of the country gets its news from the Internet, so it's no surprise that businesses have been spending less on print and broadcast ads and more on digital marketing.[301] Last year the research company eMarketer forecast that spending on digital ads would outstrip outlays on traditional ones, and much of that increase would come from amounts previously spent on print advertising. [302]

The shift has been disastrous for newspapers; advertising revenues dropped from $49 billion in 2005 to $25 billion in 2012, and the Pew Research Center estimated they dropped again to $14 billion in 2018.[303] Even traditional news outlets with digital sites say the loss of advertising revenue has been crippling. Part of the reason for the decline, publishers say, is that platforms like Facebook and Google – which together earn more than half of all digital ad dollars – share only a fraction of the ad revenue.[304] Publishers pay the cost of reporting the news, and they want a larger share of the profits.

Google says that news outlets receive more than 70 percent of the revenue generated from ads on their sites and that news outlets benefit when search engines send readers to their sites. If publishers were getting a raw deal, some tech analysts say, they would hide their content behind a paywall.

Newspapers counter they receive substantially less than 70 percent of the revenue and repeat a News Media Alliance study that found Google earns $4.7 billion from news content. [305] They also worry that a single algorithm change will obscure their sites, putting them out of business.[306] [307]

Few individual news organizations have the power to negotiate with the digital behemoths for better compensation, so the News Media Alliance drafted a measure allowing publishers to combine efforts without the threat of prosecution for violating antitrust laws. The bill is sponsored by Rep. David Cicilline, D-R.I., chairman of the House Judiciary Committee's Anti-Trust Subcommittee. His Journalism Competition and Preservation Act gives publishers a four-year safe haven while they negotiate with large platforms.[308]

Cicilline first filed the bill in 2018, but the measure didn't gain traction until last year, when a bipartisan group of co-sponsors signed on, and Sens. John Kennedy, R-La., and Amy Klobuchar, D-Minn., filed a companion bill in the Senate.[309] [310] Libertarian Sen. Rand Paul, an opponent of antitrust laws, agreed to co-sponsor the bill. According to the News Media Alliance's Danielle Coffey, Paul "loved the market-based approach."[311]

The bill's prospects were immeasurably improved earlier this year when Senate Majority Leader Mitch McConnell agreed to become a co-sponsor, reportedly after speaking with a friend who runs Kentucky's Bowling Green Daily News.

Support for the bill also has been buoyed by "techlash," the growing public sentiment that tech giants must be held responsible for privacy violations and disinformation as well as their impact on local media.[312] Rep. Cicilline's antitrust subcommittee, the Federal Trade Commission, state attorneys general and the U.S. Department of Justice are all conducting investigations, and lawsuits against Google reportedly are imminent.[313] [314]

International pressure is mounting as well. After several ill-fated European attempts to force Google to pay publishers, France's competition regulators have ordered the tech giant to negotiate with local publishers over licensing fees. Australia will soon require Google and Facebook to compensate publishers to reuse their content.[315]

Cicilline's staff reports that it will wrap up its investigation later this year and expects that the congressman will strengthen his bill by ensuring local media have a seat at the negotiating table.[316] [317] As currently written, the bill is silent on negotiation details, and local outlets worry that large national organizations could dominate.

There's a real question of how much local news outlets will benefit if the bill passes. Walter Hussman, who publishes the Arkansas Democrat-Gazette and over a dozen other local papers, says digital marketing changed the business. "There used to be a limited number of places you can run a print ad. Now there are hundreds of places that sell ads at cheaper rates." Competition has pushed rates so low that advertising revenues simply can't sustain a newsroom. As a result, Hussman says, negotiations with the platforms won't yield enough to make a significant difference to most newsrooms.

Some industry analysts, including Nieman Lab's Ken Doctor, think success will be limited because publishers need the platforms more than tech giants need news. According to Doctor, around 85 percent of publishers' external traffic comes from Google or Facebook, but only 4 percent of Facebook's News Feed posts include news.[318] So even if publishers get together and tell the platforms, "Give us x cents for every story," big tech will say, "No deal; we don't need your content." Then some publishers will break ranks rather than lose search engine audiences.

Still, Doctor believes tech dollars could make newspapers both more viable and more valuable, potentially more inviting to investment firms.[319] The president of Alden Global Capital, a company known as the "Destroyer of Newspapers," recently announced he'd like some of those tech payments. In a letter shared on Twitter by New York Times correspondent Ben Smith, Alden's President Heath Freeman comments without irony, "Fees from those who use and profit from our content can help us continually optimize our product as well as ensure our newsrooms have the resources they need."[320]

Broadcast Consolidation and Diversity: The Federal Communications Commission

While local newspapers have been struggling to survive, television stations have been thriving – at least up until the pandemic. Stations have been the beneficiaries of a seemingly limitless supply of spending on political campaigns, thanks in part to the Supreme Court's decision in Citizens United. That revenue is so significant that it's bolstered the value of stations in markets with highly contested races, particularly those in swing states.

Stations also earn hefty retransmission fees – payments from cable and satellite companies that carry their programming. According to Robert Papper, who conducts a station survey, these account for nearly 40 percent of station revenue.[321]

Flush station coffers have been good for local news. Papper's survey finds local television news production is at an all-time high.[322] But the profitability of some stations has also made them attractive acquisitions for large media companies like Sinclair Broadcasting, Tegna Inc. and Hearst Corp. The Federal Communications Commission has given the go-ahead to a number of mergers and consolidations.

Proponents of consolidation, including current FCC Chairman Ajit Pai, argue that the mergers create economies of scale, helping broadcast and print outlets survive in the digital age. Pai says "cross-owned" television stations produce more local news than comparable "noncross-owned stations" and argues that less-stringent ownership rules will allow TV stations to bail out struggling newspapers.[323]

Pai believes more consolidation would be even better. The FCC has tried to loosen ownership rules several times over the past two decades, but its rulings have been overturned in court.

Former FCC Commissioner Michael Copps says the commission has encouraged hundreds of deals, but the consolidations have "cut the muscle out of deep-dive reporting" and closed newsrooms.[324] He worries that FCC's desire to bless acquisitions has compromised its mission to protect localism, diversity and competition.

"Right now public funding at the state and municipal level is a real hard ask. It's going to require some kind of federal government intervention; the problem is way too big."

Journalists and publishers are divided over the issue. It's true that large stations produce more local news than smaller ones, and the News Media Alliance says broadcasters can help save papers. But advocacy groups say consolidation means small communities won't be covered. They also worry about editorial independence of acquired stations; it's hard to ignore Sinclair Broadcasting's now infamous corporate mandate requiring all its anchors to read the same conservative political script.[325]

The FCC's most recent rule change occurred in 2017. In a politically controversial move, the commission's Republican appointees overrode objections by the Democratic minority, paving the way for more common ownership of television and radio stations as well as increased common control of stations and newspapers. The FCC also relaxed restrictions on ownership of top-four television stations within the same market.

The Third Circuit Court of Appeals again vacated the changes, saying the FCC had not adequately considered the effect its "sweeping rule changes" would have on ownership by women and racial minorities. Chairman Pai announced he would appeal the ruling, and on April 17, the solicitor general petitioned the Supreme Court to hear the case.[326]

Several broadcasters and newspaper publishers joined the FCC in requesting Supreme Court review.[327] The News Media Alliance and the National Association of Broadcasters are among the petitioners. So is Sinclair Broadcast Group, which reportedly now hopes to purchase papers in many major markets where it owns stations.[328]

While the saga of FCC's rule changes plays out in court, several members of Congress are trying to influence the FCC through legislation. Rep. Jared Huffman, D-Calif., wants to limit consolidation by curtailing the reach of any given broadcaster. His Local and Independent Television Protection Act eliminates the FCC's so-called UHF discount, an accounting rule that allows a company to double the number of these stations it controls.[329]

The discount was once necessary because the UHF signal was typically less powerful than VHF. The discount took this into account, allowing companies to own more UHF stations before hitting a national cap on the number of households they could reach. The conversion from analog to digital eliminated the distinction between signals, and the Obama FCC eliminated the discount. Chairman Pai reintroduced it, making critics worry that he was paving the way for Sinclair Broadcasting to merge with Tribune Media Co.

Huffman first introduced his bill in 2017, after Pai's FCC reintroduced the discount. The FCC ultimately rejected the Sinclair merger, however, and the bill never made it out of committee. Huffman reintroduced his bill in the 116th Congress, but it hasn't moved.

Several representatives are worried about the lack of diversity among station owners, and they've sponsored bills to force the commission to better address the issue.[330] Late last year, the House Energy and Commerce Committee held hearings on the diversity bills, and it looked like the committee was ready to move forward.

The most expansive proposal, sponsored by Rep. G.K. Butterfield, D-N.C., re-establishes a tax certificate program that allows owners to defer taxes when they sell their stations to women and minorities.[331] A similar certificate program was in place from 1978 to 1995, and was credited with growing minority ownership.[332] But the program also encouraged sham sales, designed to take advantage of the tax breaks. Congress canceled the program just as Viacom was set to receive deferrals worth millions and the U.S. Supreme Court struck down race-based initiatives.[333]

Butterfield's staff says his bill avoids the problems of the earlier tax certificate program. It says his bill is narrowly

A RANGE OF BILLS REQUIRING FCC ACTION

Proposals to limit consolidation, increase diversity and localism

Bill	What It Proposes	Status
The Local and Independent Television Protection Act of 2019 Sponsored by Rep. Jared Huffman (D-CA)	Limits the number of households a broadcaster can reach, thus limiting corporate consolidation	Has not made progress since it was filed on March 14, 2019
Expanding Broadcast Ownership Opportunities Act of 2019 Sponsored by Rep. G.K. Butterfield (D-NC)	Reestablishes the Tax Certificate Program, which encourages station sales to minority owners Requires FCC to recommend ways to increase minority and women station owners Requires FCC to establish an incubator program to promote minority and women station ownership	Forwarded to full Energy and Commerce Committee on March 10, 2020
Enhancing Broadcaster Diversity Data Act Sponsored by Rep. Yvette Clarke (D-NY)	Directs the FCC to complete broadcast and cable EEOC rulemaking Improves broadcast ownership data collection	Forwarded to full Energy and Commerce Committee on March 10, 2020
Media Diversity Act of 2020 Sponsored by Rep. Billy Long (R-MO.)	Requires the FCC to consider market entry barriers for "socially disadvantaged individuals in the communications marketplace	Forwarded to full Energy and Commerce Committee on March 10, 2020

Source: Congress.gov

tailored to steer clear of constitutional problems, and it requires purchasers to hold stations for two years, thus discouraging fraudulent transactions. But Butterfield's office acknowledges that the bill has yet to attract needed Republican support.

Several of the bills, including Butterfield's, require the FCC to increase its reporting on diversity among station owners. The Enhancing Broadcaster Diversity Act, introduced by Rep. Yvette Clarke, D-N.Y., requires the commission to collect and analyze data on diversity. It also directs the FCC to complete its rulemaking on equal employment opportunity rules, which has been on hold for over two decades.[334] The MEDIA Diversity Act, introduced by Rep. Billy Long, R-Mo., requires the commission to report on barriers to ownership by socially disadvantaged individuals.[335] His is the only bill with Republican support.

A House Energy and Commerce Committee subcommittee advanced all three measures in early March. But they've been stalled while Congress focuses on COVID response. Staffers now think the bills are unlikely to get much attention for the remainder of the year.

Efforts to Slow or Reverse Consolidation

The Great Recession ushered in the era of a new kind of media baron: private investment entities whose primary goal was the maximization of return on investment.[336] As newspaper advertising and subscription revenues dropped, private equity firms and hedge funds snapped up distressed properties, consolidating ownership. By the end of 2014, six of the 10 largest newspaper chains were investment firms, which owned 1,039 papers, including 348 dailies and 691 weeklies. Those numbers began declining in 2017, as two of the smallest private equity firms sold their newspapers.

Today, four large firms own 15 percent of the country's papers: the private equity firm Apollo Global Management, hedge funds Chatham Asset Management and Alden Global Capital, and Fortress Investment Group, a diversified firm that manages both private equity and hedge funds.

The era of consolidation has been marked by shuttered papers and hollowed-out newsrooms. Alden Global Capital earned the nickname "Destroyer of Newspapers" for selling off assets, cutting staff and loading papers up with so much debt that bankruptcy becomes inevitable. Alden insists it is saving newspapers already in decline, but according to The Washington Post, it manages to eke out profits that are substantially higher than those of other newspaper chains.

Several members of Congress have called out the hedge fund. "Alden has pursued a strategy of acquiring newspapers, cutting staff and then selling off the real estate assets of newsrooms and printing presses at a profit," Senate Minority Leader Chuck Schumer, D-N.Y., wrote, publicly demanding to know what Alden would do if it acquired Gannett.[337] "Alden Global Capital must reverse course and put an end to policies that have hollowed out local newspapers," wrote Illinois Democratic Sens. Dick Durbin and Tammy Duckworth earlier this year as the hedge fund prepared to take over Tribune Publishing.[338]

Steve Waldman of Report for America wants to "uproot" chain-owned papers and "replant" them as locally owned nonprofit news organizations.[339] To do this, he would offer large tax deductions to companies willing to divest themselves of newspapers, then ease the paper's transition to nonprofit status.

Waldman would also create a well-endowed "deconsolidation fund," which would offer bankruptcy lawyers and transition capital to foundering newsrooms. Funding would come from Congress, philanthropy or some combination.

Sen. Elizabeth Warren, D-Mass., last summer filed a bill to curtail the ability of private equity firms to force debt onto their target companies while laying off workers. The Stop Wall Street Looting Act includes provisions that, among other things, require firms to share responsibility for the debts of the companies under their control and prevents them from sucking capital out of target firms by delaying capital distributions. The bill also increases bankruptcy protections for employee pay and severance.

Warren's staff was unavailable to comment on her bill, but an economist who analyzed the bill for her office believes it will have a limited impact on newspapers.[340] Eileen Appelbaum, the co-director of the Center for Economic and Policy Research, says increased bankruptcy protections for workers apply regardless of ownership, but many of the bill's other provisions apply only to private equity funds, not hedge funds like Alden. "Hedge funds are governed by other rules," she says. "If the company is governed by rules covering publicly traded companies, then the Stop Wall Street Looting Act won't help." [341]

Private equity firms launched an advertising campaign against the bill, and the U.S. Chamber of Commerce, Washington's biggest lobbying shop, says it will cost millions of U.S. jobs.[342] Neither Warren's bill nor its companion bill in the House has moved since they were filed last summer. One Bloomberg Law analyst noted, however, that if Democrats win big in November, many of the bill's provisions will likely earn serious consideration.[343]

Direct Government Support: State Funding

"Things are so bad, we need an all-of-the-above approach," says PEN America's Viktorya Vilk. "It can't just be federal funds; we're pushing governors to include financial support for local media in their pandemic plans."

Vilk is not alone. The Colorado Media Project, a community foundation-funded effort, wants Colorado to support public-private partnerships that will give grants to local news outlets. Both Vilk and the Colorado Media Project look to New Jersey's Civic Information Forum as a model of state engagement.[344]

The forum was the brainchild of Free Press' Mike Rispoli. But, as Rispoli can tell you, getting state aid is difficult in the best of times. He worked for years to persuade New Jersey to fund local journalism, then watched as his ambitious initiative was whittled down to 2 percent of its original size. After years on the drawing board, the Civic Information Forum finally got its start earlier this year. Then its funding was frozen when New Jersey's revenues fell victim to the pandemic.[345] But despite all the setbacks, Rispoli succeeded in persuading lawmakers to create the forum, and his experience is instructive.

"New Jersey is a news desert," Rispoli says, explaining how he became a community activist for local news. The state was once reliant on community papers, but then Gannett went on a shopping spree in 2016, purchasing many smaller chains, including the News Jersey Media Group, which owned The Record and three dozen smaller papers in New Jersey. People were hungry for good information, but they asked, "Why should I pay for this paper when Gannett stopped covering my community?"

When Rispoli learned New Jersey would receive a billion-dollar windfall from the 2017 sale of unused television spectrum, he lobbied lawmakers for $100 million to fund a nonprofit grant-making organization to support local journalists. To prevent funders from influencing the projects, Rispoli designated five state colleges and universities that would work together to create the charitable organization. The nonprofit would have its own staff but would be governed by a large board whose members are variously appointed by the governor, the legislature, community organizations and institutions of higher learning, so no group would have an inordinate influence.

The legislature approved the project. Rispoli attributes its success to a groundswell of community support for local news, fostered during his years of advocacy. The Senate majority leader backed the bill, perhaps because her local paper, The Record in northern New Jersey, was decimated by layoffs after it was purchased by Gannett.

The spectrum sale ultimately netted only $332 million, however, and Gov. Chris Christie used all but $10 million to plug holes in the state budget. So Rispoli revamped the proposal so that it called for only $5 million. By the time the legislature approved the revised project, the money was gone. Finally, late last year, a new governor found $2 million, and a board was formed. Rispoli expected funds would begin to flow. Then the pandemic again emptied state coffers.

Rispoli hopes the organization will eventually receive an annual appropriation. But as his experience has shown, state funding can be unreliable. That's especially true now as the COVID recession wrecks state budgets, forcing dramatic cuts. State shortfalls, projected at 15 percent this year, will likely be worse in the 2021 fiscal year.[346] [347] New Jersey has frozen all discretionary spending, and Colorado expects its revenues will fall by almost a quarter. Since almost all states have balanced budget requirements, there will likely be hard-to-make cuts even if federal help arrives.

Rispoli is philosophic. "The pandemic is accelerating structural problems with local news … There is no amount of 'please subscribe to this paper' that will help. … Right now public funding at the state and municipal level is a real hard ask. It's going to require some kind of federal government intervention; the problem is way too big."

THE PATH FORWARD:
Reinventing Local News

I n three turbulent months in 2020, our country has confronted three historic crises – a once-in-a century pandemic, an economic downturn of Depression-era proportions, and massive civil unrest and protests that harken back to the 1960s. Each played out on a national and international level, but also locally. Separately and together, these crises have reinforced the critical need for reliable information that guides the decisions we make every day – decisions that determine the quality of our own lives, those of our neighbors and fellow citizens, and those that will influence the lives of future generations.

As this report makes clear, we are at a moment of reckoning. The local news ecosystem is in peril. The first section, "The News Landscape in 2020," lays out what we have lost. This second section, "The News Landscape of the Future," lays out the challenges and opportunities in four interrelated categories. Now we must decide what to save, and what must be reinvented.

Journalistic Mission

News deserts contribute to cultural, economic and political divides in our increasingly polarized country. Over the past 15 years, the nation has lost a fourth of our local newspapers, which have historically been the prime source of credible and critical news and information in most small and mid-sized communities. Many of the inner-city neighborhoods, suburban towns and rural villages that have lost a newspaper are struggling economically, with as much as a third of residents living in poverty. Many are also home to large ethnic and minority populations who are often overlooked by the journalists at mainstream news organizations. "In the best case, we are undercovered. In the worst case, we are ignored," says Hilda Gurdian, publisher of a weekly newspaper covering the Latino community in North Carolina.

The nation is moving inexorably toward a date in the fourth decade of this century when whites will become a minority population in this country. Without strong local news coverage, the voices of residents in overlooked and underserved communities are not heard, and their stories are not told – to the detriment of democracy and society. Many of the communities that have lost newspapers have no alternative source of reliable local news, such as digital outlets or regional television, which are mostly clustered in affluent metro areas.

Strong local journalism builds trust in democratic institutions and it builds strong communities. In a 2018 column in The Washington Post, "The Local News Crisis is Destroying What a Divided America Desperately Needs: Common Ground," media critic Margaret Sullivan wrote, "One of the problems of losing local coverage is that we never know what we don't know. Corruption can flourish, taxes can rise, public officials can indulge their worst impulses."[348] In the early decades of the 20th century, journalists focused on establishing codes of conduct built around objectivity and fairness. Making certain that no community is disenfranchised because its residents lack access to critical information is the journalistic challenge of the 21st century. The burden for accomplishing this mission is not only on journalists, but also on community activists, philanthropists, owners of news organizations and government officials to make sure newsrooms have the resources they need to enfranchise everyone.

Business Model

Rethinking journalistic principles necessarily involves reinventing the business model. The collapse of the commercial model that sustained most newspapers, large and small, for 200 years has caused legacy and start-up news organizations to scramble to find new sources of revenue, including digital subscriptions, memberships, crowdsourcing and nonprofit grants. But so far, no silver bullet has emerged, nor is it likely that any single source of new revenue can adequately compensate for the loss of advertising dollars. As a result, local newspapers have turned to round after round of dramatic cost-cutting, which has, in turn, led to the loss of half of newspaper journalists over the past decade. Overall newsroom employment – which includes journalists working for television and digital outlets – has decreased by a fourth.

Locally owned and operated news outlets located in more affluent communities have much better prospects of cobbling together for-profit and nonprofit funding from a variety of sources than those in economically struggling communities. While some deep-pocketed benefactors have purchased larger, well-known newspapers – or financed the start-up of a local or statewide digital site – hundreds of other dailies and weeklies in less affluent, small and mid-sized communities have been shuttered when no one stepped forward to either buy the paper or support the establishment of an alternative news source. Furthermore, asking residents in poor communities to pay more for the news they receive – in order to compensate for the loss of advertising revenue – has the far-ranging consequence of exacerbating the chasm between communities that can afford quality journalism and those whose residents cannot.

Journalism is considered a "public good" because, in theory, better informed citizens make better decisions about important matters than enhance their own lives and their neighbors'. Yet, the United States is unique among democracies in its lack of government support for public media. Even the country's public broadcasting mainstays – PBS and NPR – rely primarily on nonprofit, not taxpayer, financial support. However, nonprofit support of local news amounts to a minuscule fraction of what is needed to replace the loss of revenue that has supported strong on-the-ground reporting. Increasingly, it appears that the only way to ensure that all communities – rich and poor – have access to critical information on vital topics, such as health and public safety, is to allocate more public funding toward local news. This means building out the journalistic model already established by NPR and PBS, which embodies editorial independence, and finding new ways to support legacy and start-up news organizations with taxpayer money.

Technological Capabilities

Ironically, in the internet age, we are a nation divided digitally between those who have access to high-speed internet and those who don't. Even in communities where broadband and wireless are available, many residents cannot afford the monthly bill to access those services. Bypassed by the technological revolution, residents of inner city neighborhoods, as well as rural communities and Native American reservations, struggle to get timely information about the spread of the coronavirus, for example, and their children are unable to participate in online instruction when schools are closed. Without a significant commitment at the local, state and federal levels to building out the digital infrastructure that will connect them with the rest of the country, these communities – many of which are poor and have large populations of minority residents – will slowly wither and die.

We are also a nation divided politically, in large part because of algorithms that determine the news and information we consume. News organizations – as well as international bad actors – rely on the metrics supplied by Facebook and Google to provide instant feedback on how widely a news article or misinformation is being shared and cited. Public service journalism – investigative and analytical reporting on matters of critical importance, such as education, the environment, politics and the economy – fails to gain traction on the internet, while sensational crime stories and offbeat features become a mainstay of our news feeds, and conspiracy theories rise to the top when we search for information.

Simultaneously, the dominance of Facebook and Google in the digital ad space has stripped news organizations of the revenue and profit needed to support strong public service journalism. Although both Google and Facebook have pledged $300 million to support local news, it does not begin to replace the local journalism that the two tech giants have destroyed. In testimony before Congress in 2018, Mark Zuckerberg billed Facebook as "a technology company where the main thing we do is have engineers and build products."[349] The insistence on being viewed as a technology company – not a media company – absolves the tech giants of making tough editorial decisions about their algorithms that determine the news and misinformation we receive on our feeds. It also allows them to avoid dealing with the financial hardships confronting local news organizations, especially the ones serving small and mid-sized communities, where residents need access to reliable news and information in order to make wise decisions that will affect the fate of the place they call home.

Policies and Regulations

Local journalism has been in dramatic decline over the past 15 years, as news organizations and journalists have disappeared. Yet, according to the Pew Research Center, almost three-quarters of people surveyed in 2019 were unaware of the financial difficulties confronting local newspapers and digital sites, and less than 15 percent had paid for a subscription over the past year. The variety of policies currently being considered and supported by legislators and government agencies in Washington, D.C., speak to an awakening at the federal level of what is at stake. Yet, as our overview of pending bills and policies points out, many of the proposals are targeted and limited in scope – and do not address the underlying fundamental issues.

In order to reinvent local news to meet the needs of the 21st century, new policies and regulations need to simultaneously acknowledge and address the interconnectedness of journalistic mission to the business model and technological capabilities. Massive consolidation in both the news and technology industries has shifted journalistic and business decision-making into the hands of a few corporate titans, who are detached from the impact their choices have on communities. Addressing these issues will be fraught with controversy in a polarized nation. In order to succeed, there needs to be a coordinated effort among government officials and ordinary citizens at the national, state and local levels.

The United States is a nation of both big cities and small towns. Only 775 cities have a population of more than 50,000, while almost 20,000 incorporated places have fewer than 5,000 people, according to the U.S. Census Bureau. Our system of governance relies on the consistent flow of reliable information to the 330 million residents of this country, regardless of whether they live in a high-rise apartment in the Manhattan borough of New York City, or on a farm near Manhattan, Kansas. In "Democracy Without Journalism," University of Pennsylvania professor Victor Pickard writes, "It is through local journalism that communities stay connected to and informed about what is happening in their backyards – especially in their schools, their governments, and other critical institutions and infrastructures. They rely on local news to find out about the quality of their environment – whether their air and water are safe – and who is running for local office and why. Yet it is precisely this kind of journalism that is quickly disappearing. If we as a society want to encourage this sort of reporting, we must find ways to support it."[350]

RATE YOUR LOCAL NEWS

What is the quality of the local news you are receiving? Does the news in your local newspaper or on social media help you to be safe and healthy? To spend your time and money wisely? To make informed decisions about candidates for local and state office?

A strong local news organization helps us as individuals solve everyday problems and unites us as a community to tackle the big ones. As we've lost newspapers and journalists over the past decade, researchers have found that both the quantity and quality of local news declined. In 2012, at the request of the Federal Communications Commission, a group of social scientists identified eight categories of critical information that residents of any community need in order to make wise quality-of-life decisions. This includes news about education, economic development, the environment and politics.

Here's your chance to evaluate how well your local news organization is providing you with critical information. We've designed a simple exercise that you can download at usnewsdeserts.com. (need web address for pdf and print version) Once you've filled out the chart, you can then compare your results with what researchers have found. Those results are listed below.

Activists and individuals at the community level have an important role to play. If you find your local news organization is providing you with a healthy diet of critical news, then support it. If not, then lobby local and corporate owners to address the news shortage.

What Researchers Have Found

Here are the general trends from recent studies of local news, including those produced by researchers at Duke University,[352] the University of North Carolina at Chapel Hill[353] and the University of Minnesota[354]:

- Newspapers, even in their diminished state, still produce more local stories that address a critical information need than any other news outlet. A Duke study of 100 mid-sized communities in 2016 found that newspapers accounted for 60 percent of stories produced in a typical week that addressed a critical information need. By comparison, only 15 percent of the stories produced by other outlets – television, radio, and online news sites – were both locally produced and met a critical information need.

- Newspapers also tend to provide a greater variety of stories that address a critical information need. Newspapers were much more likely, for example, to produce stories about education and politics than either television or social media, according to a UNC study of the state's news outlets in 2019.

- Television and social media news stories tended to skew heavily toward one critical information category – emergencies and public safety, including crime. Many of those were breaking news stories that did not provide context and analysis.

- The vast majority of the stories produced by regional television stations focus on newsworthy events, issues or people in the city where the station is located. Fewer than 10 percent of the stories are about events or issues outside the metro area, and almost all of those are human-interest features.

- Online outlets are still relatively rare in mid-sized communities. They produced only 10 percent of the 16,000 news stories in the Duke survey.

- One in five of the 100 mid-sized communities surveyed by Duke in 2016 had no locally produced news that addressed any of the critical information needs. Those under-served communities tended to have large Hispanic or Latino populations and be close to major metro areas.

How to Fill In the Chart

To begin, choose one or more of the news sources you typically consult. Over a period of four days, track the number of local stories produced in each category. To keep it simple, tally only the top stories on the home page of a website, the front page of a newspaper, or the morning/evening newscast you typically watch.

As an example, consider a story on the front page of your newspaper about an upcoming meeting of the local school board to discuss standardized test results. You will be answering these four questions to assess both the quality and quantity of news about the meeting.

- How many local stories were about the school board meeting on this particular day? Assuming there is only one, you would enter a 1 or a check mark in the column marked "education." If there are two stories you would enter a 2, and then answer the following questions about both stories:

- Was the story about the upcoming meeting produced by a local journalist? (For example, was there a byline on the story about the meeting?) If so, you would enter a 1 or check mark for each bylined story.

- Did the story provide you with useful facts and information? (For example: the time and date of the school board meeting) Enter a 1 or a check mark if the story or stories provide basic information.

- Did the story provide context and/or analysis that could inform your decision-making? (For example, did the story discuss local testing results from previous years and provide comparisons to other schools in the district, as well as to statewide averages.) If the story provided useful context and analysis, then enter a 1 or a check mark.

- If you are using numerals, you can add up the total score. The higher the score, the higher the quality of the story or stories in that category.

EXAMPLE OF RATING CHART THAT CAN BE DOWNLOADED AT USNEWSDESERTS.COM

Name of News Organization								
Categories	Emergencies & public safety	Health	Education	Transportation systems	Environment & planning	Economic Development	Civic Information	Political life
Examples	*Dangerous weather, accidents, crime*	*Quality of hospitals, spread of disease, availability of tests/ treatments*	*Quality of local schools, public funding, decision making processes*	*Road conditions, mass transit, future needs*	*Quality of air water, alerts to current/ potential hazards*	*Major isues at local/state level, local employment*	*Social services, religious and non profit groups, libraries*	*Voting/ candidates, major issues, public meetings*
Day 1								
Number of local stories about the topic								
Number of stories by a local journalist								
Number of stories with useful i-on								
Number of stories with valuable content analysis								
Total								

CITATIONS

1   Kristen Hare, "The Coronavirus Has Closed More Than 25 Local Newsrooms." Poynter Institute, 2020poynter.org/locally/2020/the-coronavirus-has-closed-more-than-25-local-newsrooms-across-america-and-counting

2   Matt DeRienzo, "A Recession, Then a Collapse," Nieman Lab, 2017, niemanlab.org/2017/12/a-recession-then-a-collapse

3   Victor Pickard, "Journalism's Market Failure Is a Crisis for Democracy," Harvard Business Review, March 12, 2020, hbr.org/2020/03/journalisms-market-failure-is-a-crisis-for-democracy

4   James Hamilton, All the News That's Fit to Sell (Princeton: Princeton University Press, 2006).

5   Knight Commission, "Crisis in Democracy: Renewing Trust in America," Aspen Institute, Aspen Digital, 2019, csreports.aspeninstitute.org/Knight-Commission-TMD/2019/report

6   Michael Aaron, "Final Edition: 3 Arkansas Newspapers Say Goodbye After Decades of Coverage," THV11, September 14, 2018, thv11.com/article/life/final-edition-3-arkansas-newspapers-say-goodbye-after-decades-of-coverage/91-594613344

7   Rex Nelson, "So Long, Siftings Herald," Arkansas Democrat-Gazette, September 12, 2018, arkansasonline.com/news/2018/sep/12/so-long-siftings-herald-20180912

8   Steven Waldman, "The Information Needs of Communities: The Changing Media Landscape in a Broadband Age," Federal Communications Commission, July 2011, transition.fcc.gov/osp/inc-report/The_Information_Needs_of_Communities.pdf

9   Penelope Muse Abernathy, Saving Community Journalism: The Path to Profitability (Chapel Hill: UNC Press, 2014)

10 Alex Jones, Losing the News: The Future of the News that Feeds Democracy (Oxford: Oxford University Press, 2011)

11 William Dill, "Growth of Newspapers in the United States," University of Kansas, March 15, 1928, kuscholarworks.ku.edu/bitstream/handle/1808/21361/dill_1928_3425151.pdf?sequence=1

12 Penelope Muse Abernathy, "UNC Newspaper Database," UNC Hussman School of Journalism, UNC-Chapel Hill, 2019, usnewsdeserts.com

13 Penelope Muse Abernathy, Saving Community Journalism: The Path to Profitability (Chapel Hill: UNC Press, 2014)

14 Penelope Muse Abernathy, "Methodology," UNC Hussman School of Journalism, UNC-Chapel Hill, 2019, usnewsdeserts.com/methodology

15 Kalea Hall, "Farewell to The Vindicator," Medium, April 17, 2020, medium.com/saying-goodbye-to-the-vindicator/farewell-to-the-vindicator-1bcf1c1a7848

16 "Income and Poverty in the United States: 2016," United States Census Bureau, September 12, 2017, census.gov/library/publications/2017/demo/p60-259.html

17 Terry Dickson, "Waycross Journal-Herald Ceases Publication," The Brunswick News, September 30, 2019, thebrunswicknews.com/news/local_news/waycross-journal-herald-ceases-publication/article_7ac58d42-09f4-5096-88c1-5cf5339ca149.html

See Also: Heather Chapman, "Daily Paper in Waycross, Georgia, Closes, Increasing the Number of 'News Desert' Counties in the State to 29 of 159," The Rural Blog, Institute for Rural Journalism and Community Issues, October 1, 2019, irjci.blogspot.com/2019/10/rural-georgia-daily-closes-increasing.html

18 "Waycross Mourns Longtime Publisher," The Blackshear Times, October 29, 2019, theblacksheartimes. com/news/waycross-mourns-longtime-publisher/article_f98c0eb4-fa7b-11e9-a540-8785c00d5f15.html

19 Rex Nelson, "So Long, Siftings Herald," Arkansas Democrat-Gazette, September 12, 2018, arkansasonline. com/news/2018/sep/12/so-long-siftings-herald-20180912

20 United States Census Bureau: Pryor Creek, Oklahoma, 2017, census.gov/quickfacts/ pryorcreekcityoklahoma

See Also: William W. Savage III, "Pryor Daily Times Closes, Locals 'Stunned' by Loss of Online Archives," nondoc.com, May 10, 2017, nondoc.com/2017/05/10/pryor-daily-times-closes-locals

21 Levi Pulkinnen, "Lessons on Going Online-Only From SeattlePI," Columbia Journalism Review, July 18, 2018, cjr.org/business_of_news/seattle-pi-online-only.php

See Also: Ron Shawgo, "News-Sentinel Is Going Digital," Journal Gazette, August 25, 2017, journalgazette. net/news/local/20170825/news-sentinel-is-going-digital

And: News-Sentinel, "Home," News-Sentinel, Accessed May 16, 2020, news-sentinel.com

22 "Ogden Newspapers Buys Some Vindicator Assets," News & Tech, September 2, 2019, newsandtech.com/ mergers_acquisitions/ogden-newspapers-buys-some-vindicator-assets/article_e21140e4-cd9c-11e9-89e1-fffcf3f0e4a2.html

23 Mahoning Matters, "Home," Mahoning Matters, Accessed May 16, 2020, mahoningmatters.com

24 Kalea Hall, "Farewell to The Vindicator," Medium, April 17, 2020, medium.com/saying-goodbye-to-the-vindicator/farewell-to-the-vindicator-1bcf1c1a7848

25 Al Cross, "CNHI Closes Weeklies in NE Ky., Will Send Subscribers Daily Once a Week; University Town 55 Miles Away Has No Paper," The Rural Blog, Institute for Rural Journalism and Community Issues, May 1, 2020, irjci.blogspot.com/2020/05/community-newspaper-holdings-closes.html

26 Ibid.

27 Kristen Hare, "The Coronavirus Has Closed More Than 25 Local Newsrooms." Poynter Institute, 2020poynter.org/locally/2020/the-coronavirus-has-closed-more-than-25-local-newsrooms-across-america-and-counting

28 Tali Arbel and Alexandra Olson, "As Gannett, GateHouse Merge, More Cuts to New England Newspapers," boston.com, August 24, 2019, boston.com/news/local-news/2019/08/24/as-gannett-gatehouse-merge-more-cuts-to-new-england-newspapers

29 Callum Borchers, "50 Mass. Newspapers Will Reportedly Consolidate Into 18," WBUR, May 31, 2019, wbur. org/bostonomix/2019/05/31/gatehouse-weekly-newspaper-consolidations

30 Paige Pfleger, "When The Local Paper Closes, Where Does The Community Turn?" National Public Radio, June 21, 2015, npr.org/2015/06/21/415199073/when-the-local-paper-closeswhere-does-the-community-turn

31 Paul Farhi, "The End Comes for Another Local Newspaper, 165 Years After It Began," The Washington Post, January 30, 2020, washingtonpost.com/lifestyle/style/the-end-comes-for-another-local-newspaper-165-years-after-it-began/2020/01/30/47c40b20-3647-11ea-bb7b-265f4554af6d_story.html

32 José Umaña, "County Officials React to Montgomery County Sentinel Closure," The Sentinel, January 30, 2020, mont.thesentinel.com/2020/01/30/county-officials-react-to-montgomery-county-sentinel-closure

33 Library of Congress, "About the Evening Press. (Carthage, Mo.) 1885–1891," Chronicling America, Library of Congress, chroniclingamerica.loc.gov/lccn/sn89066634

See Also: Tyler Wornell, "Carthage Press to Close After 134 Years of Operation," The Joplin Globe, August 29, 2018, joplinglobe.com/news/update-carthage-press-to-close-after-years-of-operation/article_2cd2f510-ab97-11e8-8069-6b585c4deb6f.html

34 Clara Hendrickson, "Critical in a Public Health Crisis, COVID-19 Has Hit Local Newsrooms Hard," Brookings, April 8, 2020, brookings.edu/blog/fixgov/2020/04/08/critical-in-a-public-health-crisis-covid-19-has-hit-local-newsrooms-hard

35 Lewis Friedland et al., "Review of the Literature Regarding Critical Information Needs of the American Public," Federal Communications Commission, July 16, 2012, transition.fcc.gov/bureaus/ocbo/Final_Literature_Review.pdf

36 Philip Napoli et al., "Assessing Local Journalism," Sanford School of Public Policy, Duke University, August 2018, dewitt.sanford.duke.edu/wp-content/uploads/2018/08/Assessing-Local-Journalism_100-Communities.pdf

37 Philip Napoli and Jessica Mahone, "Local Newspapers Are Suffering, but They're Still (by Far) the Most Significant Journalism Producers in Their Communities," Nieman Lab, September 9, 2019, niemanlab.org/2019/09/local-newspapers-are-suffering-but-theyre-still-by-far-the-most-significant-journalism-producers-in-their-communities

See Also: Jessica Mahone et al., "Who's Producing Local Journalism: Assessing Journalistic Output Across Different Outlet Types," Sanford School of Public Policy, Duke University, August, 2019, dewitt.sanford.duke.edu/whos-producing-local-journalism-nmrp-report

38 Pengjie Gao, Chang Lee, Dermot Murphy, "Financing Dies in Darkness? The Impact of Newspaper Closures on Public Finance" (August 10, 2018). Available at SSRN: ssrn.com/ abstract=3175555 or dx.doi.org/10.2139/ssrn.3175555

39 Rural and nonrural classification is derived from United States Department of Agriculture's RuralUrban Continuum Codes (RUCC) definition of metro and nonmetro. Metro counties include counties that fall within RUCC 1-3 while nonmetro counties fall within RUCC 4-9. ers.usda.gov/data-products/rural-urban-continuum-codes/documentation

40 "Income and Poverty in the United States: 2016," United States Census Bureau, September 12, 2017, census.gov/library/publications/2017/demo/p60-259.html

41 James Hamilton and Fiona Morgan, "Poor Information: How Economics Affects the Information Lives of Low-Income Individuals," International Journal of Communication, 12 (2018): ijoc.org/index.php/ijoc/article/view/8340

42 States were grouped into regions according to the following classifications: Pacific: AK, CA, HI, OR, WA; Mountain: AZ, CO, ID, MT, NM, NV, UT, WY; Midwest: IA, IL, IN, KS, MI, MN, MO, ND, NE, OH, SD, WI; Mid-Atlantic: NJ, NY, PA; South: AL, AR, DC, DE, FL, GA, KY, LA, MD, MS, NC, OK, SC, TN, TX, VA, WV ; New England: CT, MA, ME, NH, RI, VT

43 Helen Branswell, "When Towns Lose Their Newspapers, Diseases Detectives Are Left Flying Blind," Stat News, March 20, 2018, statnews.com/2018/03/20/news-deserts-infectious-disease

44 Viola Gienger, "Coronavirus, Public Perceptions and the Dangers of 'News Deserts,' " Just Security, March 25, 2020, justsecurity.org/69337/coronavirus-public-perceptions-and-the-dangers-of-news-deserts

45 Jim Conaghan, Interview with Penny Abernathy discussing digital and print readership, May 02, 2016

46 Elizabeth Grieco, "U.S. Newspapers Have Shed Half of Their Newsroom Employees Since 2008," FactTank,

Pew Research Center, April 20, 2020, pewresearch.org/fact-tank/2020/04/20/u-s-newsroom-employment-has-dropped-by-a-quarter-since-2008

47 Steven Smethers, "Silent 'Signal': Baldwin City Adjusts to Life Without a Newspaper," Kansas State University presentation, April 11, 2018.

48 Amy Maestas, "Ann Arbor: Citizenship and the Local Newspaper," 2017, Thwarting the Emergence of News Deserts, UNC-Chapel Hill. See also: Sarah Cavanah, "Measuring Metropolitan Newspaper Pullback and Its Effects on Political Participation," 2016, Retrieved from the University of Minnesota Digital Conservancy, hdl.handle.net/11299/182213

49 Penelope Muse Abernathy, Saving Community Journalism: The Path to Profitability (Chapel Hill: UNC Press, 2014)

50 Tom Rosenstiel and Amy Mitchell, "The State of the News Media, 2011," Pew Research Center, 2011, pewresearch.org/wp-content/uploads/sites/8/2017/05/State-of-the-News-Media-Report-2011-FINAL.pdf

    See Also: John Gramlich, "Q&A: What Pew Research Center's New Survey Says About Local News in the U.S.," FactTank, Pew Research Center, March 26, 2019, pewresearch.org/fact-tank/2019/03/26/qa-what-pew-research-centers-new-survey-says-about-local-news-in-the-u-s

51 Jolie O'Dell, "For the First Time, More People Get News Online Than From Newspapers," Mashable, March 14, 2011, mashable.com/2011/03/14/online-versus-newspaper-news

52 Todd Haselton, "More Americans Now Get News From Social Media Than From Newspapers, Says Survey," CNBC, December 10, 2018, cnbc.com/2018/12/10/social-media-more-popular-than-newspapers-for-news-pew.html

53 Information on distribution of newspapers from Standard Rate and Data Service, Print Media Circulation, 1992

    And: Information on distribution of newspapers from Standard Rate and Data Service, Print Media Circulation, 2018

54 Ibid.

55 Mason Walker, "Who Pays for Local News in the U.S.?" FactTank, Pew Research Center, September 12, 2019, pewresearch.org/fact-tank/2019/09/12/who-pays-for-local-news-in-the-u-s

56 Hsiang Iris Chyi and Yee Man Margaret Ng, "Still Unwilling to Pay: An Empirical Analysis of 50 U.S. Newspapers' Digital Subscription Results," Digital Journalism (March, 2020), tandfonline.com/eprint/DFGQGBYDC3CV3UZ3RHQP/full?target=10.1080/21670811.2020.1732831

57 Penelope Muse Abernathy and Joann Sciarrino, The Strategic Digital Media Entrepreneur, (Hoboken: Wiley Blackwell, 2019)

58 Alex Jones, Losing the News: The Future of the News That Feeds Democracy, (Oxford, Oxford University Press, 2011)

59 Elizabeth Grieco, "U.S. Newspapers Have Shed Half of Their Newsroom Employees Since 2008," FactTank, Pew Research Center, April 20, 2020, pewresearch.org/fact-tank/2020/04/20/u-s-newsroom-employment-has-dropped-by-a-quarter-since-2008

60 Philip Napoli et al., "Assessing Local Journalism," Sanford School of Public Policy, Duke University, August, 2018, dewitt.sanford.duke.edu/wp-content/uploads/2018/08/Assessing-Local-Journalism_100-Communities.pdf

61 Tom Jones, "Why Did It Take So Long for the Ahmaud Arbery Shooting to Become One of the Biggest Stories in the Country?" Poynter, May 12, 2020, poynter.org/newsletters/2020/why-did-it-take-so-long-

for-the-ahmaud-arbery-shooting-to-become-one-of-the-biggest-stories-in-the-country

62   Charles Bethea, "What Happens When the News Is Gone?" The New Yorker, January 27, 2020, newyorker.com/news/the-future-of-democracy/what-happens-when-the-news-is-gone

63   Joe Nocera, "Alden Global Capital's Business Model Destroys Newspapers for Little Gain," Bloomberg, March 26, 2018, bloombergquint.com/view/alden-global-capital-s-business-model-destroys-newspapers-for-little-gain

64   Anna Clark, "The Last Days of the Cleveland Plain Dealer Newsroom," Columbia Journalism Review, May 13, 2020, cjr.org/analysis/advance-local-one-cleveland-plain-dealer-layoffs.php

65   James Hamilton, Democracy's Detectives (Boston: Harvard University Press, 2016)

66   James Hamilton, Democracy's Detectives (Boston: Harvard University Press, 2016)

67   Sarah Cavanah, "Measuring Metropolitan Newspaper Pullback and Its Effects on Political Participation," Retrieved from the University of Minnesota Digital Conservancy, 2016, hdl.handle.net/11299/182213

68   Tom Jones, "A Brunswick Reporter Talks About the Ahmaud Arbery Shooting: 'It Didn't Smell Good From the Start,'" Poynter, March 14, 2020, poynter.org/newsletters/2020/a-brunswick-reporter-talks-about-the-ahmaud-arbery-shooting-it-didnt-smell-good-from-the-start

69   Interview with Jon Schleuss, President, NewsGuild, March 29, 2020

70   James Hamilton, Democracy's Detectives (Boston: Harvard University Press, 2016)

71   Ibid

72   The New York Times Company, "The New York Times Company Reports 2019 Fourth-Quarter and Full-Year Results and Announces Dividend Increase," New York Times Company, February 6, 2020, investors.nytco.com/investors/investor-news/investor-news-details/2020/The-New-York-Times-Company-Reports-2019-Fourth-Quarter-and-Full-Year-Results-and-Announces-Dividend-Increase/default.aspx

73   Mark Anderson, "McClatchy Eliminating Saturday Print Editions in More Markets," Sacramento Business Journal, June 6, 2019, bizjournals.com/sacramento/news/2019/06/06/mcclatchy-eliminating-saturday-printeditions-in.html

74   David Bockino, "Three Days a Week: Has A New Production Cycle Altered The Times-Picayune's News Coverage?" Paper presented at the annual meeting of the Association for Education in Journalism and Mass Communication, Renaissance Hotel, Washington DC, Aug 08, 2013

75   Samantha Sunne, "The Times-Picayune Was Absorbed by the Advocate in New Orleans Yesterday. Here's What Happened to Its Staff," Poynter, July 1, 2019, poynter.org/business-work/2019/the-times-picayune-was-absorbed-by-the-advocate-in-new-orleans-yesterday-heres-what-happened-to-its-staff

76   Mark Jacob, "The Arkansas Gamble: Can a Tablet and a Print Replica Rescue Local News?" Local News Initiative, Northwestern, January 13, 2020, localnewsinitiative.northwestern.edu/posts/2020/01/13/arkansas-democrat-gazette-tablet

77   Paul Tash, "Pandemic Prompts Change in Newspaper Delivery at Tampa Bay Times," Tampa Bay Times, March 30, 2020, tampabay.com/news/business/2020/03/30/pandemic-prompts-change-in-newspaper-delivery-at-tampa-bay-times

78   Penelope Muse Abernathy, "One Publisher's Story: 'We Need to Diversify,'" Center For Innovation and Sustainability in Local Media, Hussman School of Journalism and Media, UNC at Chapel Hill, 2019, cislm.

org/digitalstrategy/sdme-chapter-10-investing-in-key-assets-and-capabilities/sdme-one-publishers-story-we-need-to-diversify

[79] Saheli Roy Choudhury, "SoftBank to Buy Fortress Investment for $3.3 Billion in Cash," CNBC, February 14, 2017, cnbc.com/2017/02/14/softbank-to-buy-fortress-investment-for-33-billion.html

[80] Rick Edmonds, "As the Gannett-GateHouse Merger Is Approved, a Long Road to Digital Transformation Remains," Poynter, November 14, 2019, poynter.org/business-work/2019/as-the-gannett-gatehouse-merger-is-approved-a-long-road-to-digital-transformation-remains/.

[81] Ibid.

[82] Fern Siegel, "Lee Enterprises Buys BH Media Group's Newspapers for $140 Million," MediaPost, PublishersDaily, January 29, 2020, mediapost.com/publications/article/346368/lee-enterprises-buys-bh-media-groups-newspapers-f.html

[83] Rick Edmonds, "Is Alden the Archvillain Crushing Local News? It's a Little More Complicated," Poynter, February 20, 2020, poynter.org/business-work/2020/is-alden-the-archvillain-crushing-local-news-its-a-little-more-complicated

[84] Kristen Hare, "Here Are the Newsroom Layoffs, Furloughs and Closures Caused by the Coronavirus," Poynter, May 15, 2020, poynter.org/business-work/2020/here-are-the-newsroom-layoffs-furloughs-and-closures-caused-by-the-coronavirus

[85] 6-month stock price for GCI (Gannett), LEE and TPCO (Tribune)

[86] Alan Mutter, "Newspaper Share Value Fell $64B in '08," Reflections of a Newsosaur, January 1, 2009, newsosaur.blogspot.com/2008/12/newspaper-share-value-fell-64b-in-08.html

[87] Transaction stats from Dirks, Van Essen, Murray and April, Year-End 2017, December 31, 2017, dirksvanessen.com/articles/view/227/year-end-2017/ and Dirks, Van Essen, Murray and April, Q2 2018, July 1, 2018, dirksvanessen.com/articles/view/231/2nd-quarter-2018/

[88] Rick Kelley, "AIM Media Buys Civitas Media Properties in Major Acquisition," Valley Morning Star, June 13, 2017, valleymorningstar.com/2017/06/13/aim-media-buys-civitas-media-properties-in-major-acquisition/

[89] "Investing in Newspapers in 2018," Key Executives Mega-Conference Panel Discussion, San Diego, February 27, 2018

[90] Robert McChesney, Communication Revolution: Critical Junctures and the Future of Media (New York: New Press, 2007)

[91] Megan Brenan, "Americans' Trust in Mass Media Edges Down to 41%," Gallup, September 26, 2019, news.gallup.com/poll/267047/americans-trust-mass-media-edges-down.aspx

See Also: Megan Brenan, "Local News Media Considered Less Biased Than National News," Gallup, November 8, 2019, news.gallup.com/poll/268160/local-news-media-considered-less-biased-national-news.aspx

[92] John Gramlich, "Q&A: What Pew Research Center's New Survey Says About Local News in the U.S.," FactTank, Pew Research Center, March 26, 2019, pewresearch.org/fact-tank/2019/03/26/qa-what-pew-research-centers-new-survey-says-about-local-news-in-the-u-s

[93] Robert McChesney, Communication Revolution: Critical Junctures and the Future of Media (New York: New Press, 2007)

[94] "Investing in Newspapers in 2018," Key Executives Mega-Conference Panel Discussion, San Diego, February 27, 2018, snpa.static2.adqic.com/static/2018MegaProgram.pdf

See Also: "Thwarting the Emergence of News Deserts," UNC Center for Innovation and Sustainability in Local Media, 2017.

And: "Hearst Acquires Print, Digital and Local Media Assets of 21st Century Media Newspaper, LLC, Including the New Haven Register," Hearst, June 5, 2017, https://www.hearst.com/-/hearst-acquires-print-digital-and-local-media-assets-of-21st-century-media-newspaper-llc-including-the-new-haven-register

95 Julie Reynolds, "Hedge Fund Alden Siphoned 100s of Millions From Newspapers in Scheme to Gamble on Other Investments, Suit Says," dfmworkers.org, March 8, 2018 dfmworkers.org/hedge-fund-alden-siphoned-100s-of-millions-from-newspapers-in-scheme-to-gamble-on-other-investments-suit-says

96 poynter.org/business-work/2019/as-the-gannett-gatehouse-merger-is-approved-a-long-road-to-digital-transformation-remains

97 Eli M. Noam, Media Ownership and Concentration in America (Oxford, Oxford University Press, 2009)

98 Penelope Muse Abernathy and Joann Sciarrino, The Strategic Digital Media Entrepreneur, (Hoboken: Wiley Blackwell, 2019)

99 poynter.org/business-work/2020/its-time-to-uproot-american-newspapers-from-hedge-funds-and-replant-them-into-more-hospitable-ground

100 Pew Center, "Newspapers Fact Sheet," Pew Research Center, July 9, 2019, journalism.org/fact-sheet/newspapers

101 John Nagy, "What a Family Owned Paper Means to a Community," in Thwarting the Emergence of News Deserts, ed. Penelope Abernathy (Chapel Hill, UNC Press, 2017)

102 Penelope Abernathy, "One Publisher's Story: 'We Need to Diversify,'" Center For Innovation and Sustainability in Local Media, Hussman School of Journalism and Media, UNC-Chapel Hill, 2019, cislm.org/digitalstrategy/sdme-chapter-10-investing-in-key-assets-and-capabilities/sdme-one-publishers-story-we-need-to-diversify

103 Penelope Muse Abernathy, Saving Community Journalism: The Path to Profitability (Chapel Hill: UNC Press, 2014)

104 Phil Wright, "EO Media Group Buys Bend Bulletin," East Oregonian, July 29, 2019, eastoregonian.com/news/local/eo-media-group-buys-bend-bulletin/article_e7907dfa-b20d-11e9-a9b2-4be6e2beadab.html

105 Research Interview with New England Newspapers Inc. President Fredric Rutberg, July 13, 2018.

106 Reed College of Media, "Five NewStart Fellows Named for New Master's Program," West Virginia University, April 28, 2020, mediacollege.wvu.edu/news/2020/04/28/five-newstart-fellows-named-for-new-masters-program

107 Penelope Muse Abernathy, Saving Community Journalism: The Path to Profitability, (Chapel Hill: UNC Press, 2014)

108 Jefferson Graham, "Legendary Chicago Defender Publication to Go Digital Only," USA Today, July 7, 2019, usatoday.com/story/money/2019/07/07/chicago-defender-cease-print-publication-go-online-only/1668023001

109 Gustavo Martínez Contreras, "Oldest Spanish Newspaper in the U.S. Struggles to Stay Afloat and Relevant," Borderzine, January 30, 2016, borderzine.com/2016/01/oldest-spanish-newspaper-in-the-u-s-struggles-to-stay-afloat-and-relevant

110 "The State of the Latino News Media," The Latino Media Report, CUNY Craig Newmark Graduate School of Journalism, June, 2019, thelatinomediareport.journalism.cuny.edu

111 Sonam Vashi, "How Mundo Hispánico, Georgia's Largest Spanish-language Newspaper, Survived a Near-Death Experience," Atlanta Magazine, March 22, 2019, atlantamagazine.com/news-culture-articles/how-

mundo-hispanico-georgias-largest-spanish-language-newspaper-survived-a-near-death-experience

[112] "The State of the Latino News Media," The Latino Media Report, CUNY Craig Newmark Graduate School of Journalism, June 2019, thelatinomediareport.journalism.cuny.edu

[113] Jodi Rave, "American Indian Media Today," Democracy Fund, November 2018, https://democracyfund.org/idea/american-indian-media-today/

[114] "The State of the Latino News Media," The Latino Media Report, CUNY Craig Newmark Graduate School of Journalism, June 2019, thelatinomediareport.journalism.cuny.edu

[115] Flint Beat, "About Us," Flint Beat, December 26, 2018, flintbeat.com/about-us

[116] "The State of the Latino News Media," The Latino Media Report, CUNY Craig Newmark Graduate School of Journalism, June, 2019, thelatinomediareport.journalism.cuny.edu

[117] Sonam Vashi, "How Mundo Hispánico, Georgia's Largest Spanish-Language Newspaper, Survived a Near-Death Experience," Atlanta Magazine, March 22, 2019, atlantamagazine.com/news-culture-articles/how-mundo-hispanico-georgias-largest-spanish-language-newspaper-survived-a-near-death-experience

[118] "The State of the Latino News Media," The Latino Media Report, CUNY Craig Newmark Graduate School of Journalism, June 2019, thelatinomediareport.journalism.cuny.edu

[119] Santa Cruz Local, "About," Santa Cruz Local, Accessed May 17, 2020, santacruzlocal.org/about

See Also: Santa Cruz Local, "Help," Santa Cruz Local, Accessed May 17, 2020, santacruzlocal.org/help

[120] Elizabeth Grieco, "U.S. Newspapers Have Shed Half of Their Newsroom Employees Since 2008," FactTank, Pew Research Center, April 20, 2020, pewresearch.org/fact-tank/2020/04/20/u-s-newsroom-employment-has-dropped-by-a-quarter-since-2008

[121] Philip Napoli and Jessica Mahone, "Local Newspapers Are Suffering, but They're Still (by Far) the Most Significant Journalism Producers in Their Communities," Nieman Lab, September 9, 2019, niemanlab.org/2019/09/local-newspapers-are-suffering-but-theyre-still-by-far-the-most-significant-journalism-producers-in-their-communities

See Also: Jessica Mahone et al., "Who's Producing Local Journalism: Assessing Journalistic Output Across Different Outlet Types," Sanford School of Public Policy, Duke University, August 2019, dewitt.sanford.duke.edu/whos-producing-local-journalism-nmrp-report

[122] Alan D. Mutter, "Op-Ed: Why Online News Sites Keep Failing," Los Angeles Times, June 25, 2015, latimes.com/opinion/op-ed/la-oe-0625-mutter-news-startups-20150625-story.html

[123] marylandreporter.com/2017/08/16/what-is-montgomery-reporter

[124] Christine Schmidt, "Want to Start Your Own Local Online News Outlet? With a New Staff and a $1 Million Grant, LION Publishers Wants to Do More to Help," Nieman Lab, December 9, 2019, niemanlab.org/2019/12/want-to-start-your-own-local-online-news-outlet-with-a-new-staff-and-a-1-million-grant-lion-publishers-wants-to-do-more-to-help

[125] Ibid

[126] Michele McLellan, Jesse Holcomb, "INN Index 2019," Institute for Nonprofit News, 2019, inn.org/innindex

[127] Matthew Nisbet et al., "Funding the News: Foundations and Nonprofit Media," Shorenstein Center on Media, Politics and Public Policy, Harvard Kennedy School, June 18, 2018, shorensteincenter.org/funding-the-news-foundations-and-nonprofit-media

[128] Knight Foundation, "Support Local," Knight Foundation, Accessed May 17, 2020, knightfoundation.org/

features/localnews

129 Interview with Laurie Paarlberg, Stewart Mott Chair in Philanthropy, Indiana University Purdue University Indianapolis, March 23, 2020

130 Matthew Nisbet et al., "Funding the News: Foundations and Nonprofit Media," Shorenstein Center on Media, Politics and Public Policy, Harvard Kennedy School, June 18, 2018, shorensteincenter.org/funding-the-news-foundations-and-nonprofit-media

131 Michele McLellan, Jesse Holcomb, "INN Index 2019," Institute for Nonprofit News, 2019, inn.org/innindex

132 Interview with Tom Shine, News Director, KMUW, March 20, 2020

133 Interview and Correspondence with Sue Cross, CEO and Executive Director, Institute for Nonprofit News, March 12, 2020, and April 29, 2020

134 Ibid

135 Pew Center, "Local TV News Fact Sheet," Pew Research Center, June 25, 2019, journalism.org/fact-sheet/local-tv-news

See Also: CPB, "About Public Media," Corporation for Public Broadcasting, Accessed May 17, 2020, cpb.org/aboutpb/what-public-media

136 Pew Center, "What Are the Local News Dynamics in Your City: Raleigh, Pinehurst, Bennington," Pew Research Center, March 26, 2019, journalism.org/interactives/local-news-habits/13540

137 Howard Husock, "Public Media Must Reimagine Itself for a New Era – Or Give Up 'Reason to Exist,'" Current, December 7, 2018, current.org/2018/12/public-media-must-reimagine-itself-for-a-new-era-or-give-up-reason-to-exist

138 CPB, "Preliminary FY 2019 Operating Budget," Corporation for Public Broadcasting, 2019, cpb.org/sites/default/files/Approved%20FY%202019%20Operating%20Budget.pdf

See Also: CPB, "Alternative Sources of Funding for Public Broadcasting Stations," Corporation for Public Broadcasting, June 20, 2012, cpb.org/files/aboutcpb/Alternative_Sources_of_Funding_for_Public_Broadcasting_Stations.pdf

And: Pew Center, "Public Broadcasting Fact Sheet," Pew Research Center, July 23, 2019, journalism.org/fact-sheet/public-broadcasting

139 Howard Husock, "Public Media Must Reimagine Itself for a New Era – Or Give Up 'Reason to Exist,'" Current, December 7, 2018, current.org/2018/12/public-media-must-reimagine-itself-for-a-new-era-or-give-up-reason-to-exist

140 Interview with Robert Papper, Director, RTDNA Annual Survey, March 22, 2020

See Also: Pew Center, "Local TV News Fact Sheet," Pew Research Center, June 25, 2019, journalism.org/fact-sheet/local-tv-news

141 Howard Husock, "Public Media Must Reimagine Itself for a New Era – Or Give Up 'Reason to Exist,' " Current, December 7, 2018, current.org/2018/12/public-media-must-reimagine-itself-for-a-new-era-or-give-up-reason-to-exist

142 Interview with Robert Papper, Director, RTDNA Annual Survey, March 22, 2020

143 NPR, "Collaborative Journalism: NPR and Member Stations Working Together," National Public Radio, Accessed May 17, 2020, npr.org/about-npr/805749582/collaborative-journalism-npr-and-member-stations-working-together

144 Interview with Tom Shine, News Director, KMUW, March 20, 2020

145 NPR, "NPR And California Public Radio Stations Collaborate On a Statewide Regional Newsroom," National Public Radio, February 6, 2020, npr.org/about-npr/803359435/npr-and-california-public-radio-stations-collaborate-on-a-statewide-regional-new

146 NPR, "Collaborative Journalism: NPR and Member Stations Working Together," National Public Radio, Accessed May 17, 2020, npr.org/about-npr/805749582/collaborative-journalism-npr-and-member-stations-working-together

147 Interview with Robert Papper, Director, RTDNA Annual Survey, March 22, 2020.

148 NPR, "Collaborative Journalism: NPR and Member Stations Working Together," National Public Radio, Accessed May 17, 2020, npr.org/about-npr/805749582/collaborative-journalism-npr-and-member-stations-working-together.

149 Matthew Nisbet et al., "Funding the News: Foundations and Nonprofit Media," Shorenstein Center on Media, Politics and Public Policy, Harvard Kennedy School, June 18, 2018, shorensteincenter.org/funding-the-news-foundations-and-nonprofit-media

150 Howard Husock, "Public Media Must Reimagine Itself for a New Era – Or Give Up 'Reason to Exist,' " Current, December 7, 2018, current.org/2018/12/public-media-must-reimagine-itself-for-a-new-era-or-give-up-reason-to-exist

151 Penelope Muse Abernathy and Richard Foster, "The News Landscape in 2014: Transformed or Diminished? (Formulating a Game Plan for Survival in the Digital Era)," Geopolitics, History & International Relations, 2, No. 2 (2016)

152 Pulitzer Prizes, "Winners by Category: Public Service," Pulitzer Prizes, Accessed May 18, 2020, pulitzer.org/ prize-winners-by-category/204

153 William H. Frey, "The US Will Become 'Minority White' in 2045, Census Projects," Brookings, September 10, 2018, brookings.edu/blog/the-avenue/2018/03/14/the-us-will-become-minority-white-in-2045-census-projects

154 M. Rodriguez, B. Horton, and K. Bammarito, Toolkit for Community Health Providers: Engaging Ethnic Media to Inform Communities about Safe Infant Sleep (Washington D.C.: National Center for Cultural Competence, Georgetown University for Child and Human Development, 2012), nccc.georgetown.edu/engaging-ethnic-media/Engaging-Ethnic-Media.pdf

155 Daniela Gerson and Carlos Rodriguez, "Going Forward: How Ethnic and Mainstream Media Can Collaborate in Changing Communities," American Press Institute, July 19, 2018, americanpressinstitute.org/publications/reports/strategy-studies/ethnic-and-mainstream-media-collaborations-in-changing-communities

156 The Black Press: Soldiers Without Swords, directed by Stanley Nelson (1999; PBS), Television Film

157 "Quick Facts: United States," United States Census Bureau, July, 2019, census.gov/quickfacts/fact/table/US/PST045219

158 William H. Frey, "As Americans Spread Out, Immigration Plays a Crucial Role in Local Population Growth," Brookings, April 22, 2019, brookings.edu/research/as-americans-spread-out-immigration-plays-a-crucial-role-in-local-population-growth

159 Kristen Bialik, "5 Facts About Blacks in the U.S.," FactTank, Pew Research Center, February 22, 2018, pewresearch.org/fact-tank/2018/02/22/5-facts-about-blacks-in-the-u-s

160 "The State of the Latino News Media," The Latino Media Report, CUNY Craig Newmark Graduate School of Journalism, June, 2019, thelatinomediareport.journalism.cuny.edu

161 Ibid

162 Elisa Shearer, "Hispanic and Black News Media Fact Sheet," Journalism & Media, Pew Research Center, July 9, 2019, journalism.org/fact-sheet/hispanic-and-black-news-media

163 Daffodil Altan, "Ethnic Media in the U.S.: A Growing Force," Frontline, PBS, February 27, 2007, pbs.org/wgbh/pages/frontline/newswar/part3/ethnic.html

164 Michael Graff, "Life Lessons: La Noticia Publisher Hilda Gurdian," Charlotte Magazine, December 26, 2016, charlottemagazine.com/life-lessons-la-noticia-publisher-hilda-gurdian

165 L.A. Sentinel 2019 Media Kit, (Los Angeles: Los Angeles Sentinel, 2019), lasentinel.net/static/pdf/2019-LASentinel-Media-Kit-v5.pdf

166 "Focusing: Why the Chicago Defender Went Digital-Only," Local News Initiative, Northwestern University, September 9, 2019, localnewsinitiative.northwestern.edu/posts/2019/09/09/news-leaders-defender

167 Jonathan Taplin, "Forget ATT. The Real Monopolies are Google and Facebook (The New York Times, Dec. 13, 2016). nytimes.com/2016/12/13/opinion/forget-att-the-real-monopolies-are-google-and-facebook.html

168 "Income Percentile by Race Calculator for 2018," DQYDJ, 2018, dqydj.com/income-percentile-by-race-calculator

169 Matthew Nisbet and John Wihbey, "Funding the News: Foundations and Nonprofit Media," Shorenstein Center on Media, Politics and Public Policy, Harvard Kennedy School, June 18, 2018, shorensteincenter.org/funding-the-news-foundations-and-nonprofit-media

170 Jodi Rave, "American Indian Media Today," Democracy Fund, December 6, 2018, democracyfund.org/publications/american-indian-media-today

171 Ibid

172 "The State of Latino News Media,"The Latino Media Report

173 "Tribune to Sell Hoy New York to ImpreMedia," InPlay Briefing, Reuters, February 12, 2007, reuters.com/article/idUSIN20070212111542TRB20070212

174 Shearer, "Hispanic and Black News Media."

175 "Tribune Publishing Closing Hoy," News & Tech, November 22, 2019, newsandtech.com/mergers_acquisitions/tribune-publishing-closing-hoy/article_f774d870-0d56-11ea-9457-279b5fda724b.html

176 "Focusing," Local News Initiative

177 "The State of Latino News Media,"The Latino Media Report;"Lupa," Radio Ambulante, NPR, accessed March 8, 2020, radioambulante.org/en/education/lupa; Eduardo Suárez, "How a podcast created a language app to better serve its audience," Reuters Institute, University of Oxford, November 12, 2019, reutersinstitute.politics.ox.ac.uk/risj-review/how-podcast-created-language-app-better-serve-its-audience

178 Nicolás Kanellos and Helvetia Martell, Hispanic Periodicals in the United States, Origins to 1960: A Brief History and Comprehensive Bibliography (Houston: Arte Publico Press, 1999)

179 Ibid

180 Juan Gonzalez and Joseph Torres, News for All the People: The Epic Story of Race and the American Media (London: Verso, 2011)

181 Charlotte O'Kelly, "Black Newspapers and the Black Protest Movement: Their Historical Relationship, 1827-1945," Phylon 43, no. 1 (1982): 1–14

182 Elizabeth James, "Toward Alaska Native Political Organization: The Origins of Tundra Times," Western Historical Quarterly 41, no. 3 (2010): 285–303

183 Sherry Yu, "Multi-ethnic public sphere and accessible ethnic media: mapping online English-language

ethnic media," Journal of Ethnic and Migration Studies 44, no. 11 (2018): 1976–1993

[184] "La Gaceta," La Gaceta Newspaper, accessed March 8, 2020, lagacetanewspaper.com

[185] Kanellos and Martell, Hispanic Periodicals

[186] Antonio Flores and Mark Hugo Lopez, "Among U.S. Latinos, the Internet Now Rivals Television as a Source for News," FactTank, Pew Research Center, January 11, 2018, pewresearch.org/fact-tank/2018/01/11/among-u-s-latinos-the-internet-now-rivals-television-as-a-source-for-news

[187] "Focusing," Local News Initiative

[188] Shearer, "Hispanic and Black News Media."

[189] Grand Forks Herald, "Other View: A World Without Newspapers? Be Serious," Duluth News Tribune, August 16,, 2017, duluthnewstribune.com/opinion/4312825-other-view-world-without-newspapers-be-serious

[190] Ricardo Sandoval-Palos, "Water for Deserts," PBS Public Editor, PBS, Last Updated March 2, 2020, pbs.org/publiceditor/blogs/pbs-public-editor/water-for-deserts

[191] Current, "Homepage," Current, Accessed April 8, 2020, current.org

[192] Julie Drizin, in discussion with the author, March 16, 2020

[193] NPR Media Relations, "NPR Maintains Highest Ratings Ever," National Public Radio, March 28, 2018, npr.org/about-npr/597590072/npr-maintains-highest-ratings-ever

[194] PBS, "About PBS," Public Broadcasting Service, Accessed April 7, 2020, pbs.org/about/about-pbs/overview

[195] CPB, "CPB Support for Rural Stations," Corporation for Public Broadcasting, Accessed April 13, 2020, cpb.org/aboutpb/rural

[196] Kerri Hoffman, (CEO, PRX) in discussion with the author, April 1, 2020

[197] "Public Broadcasting Act of 1967." Encyclopedia.comencyclopedia.com/history/ecncyclopedias-almanacs-transcripts-and-maps/public-broadcasting-act-1967

[198] Kerri Hoffman (CEO, PRX) in discussion with the author, April 1, 2020

[199] FCC, "Overview," Federal Communications Commission, Accessed April 7, 2020, fcc.gov

[200] Kerri Hoffman (CEO, PRX) in discussion with the author, April 1, 2020

[201] Alan Yu, "Love It or Hate It, Truckers Say They Can't Stop Listening to Public Radio," Current, August 21, 2017, current.org/2017/08/love-it-or-hate-it-truckers-say-they-cant-stop-listening-to-public-radio

[202] Adam Ragusea, "Topple the Towers: Why Public Radio and Television Stations Should Radically Reorient Toward Digital-First Local News, and How They Could Do It," Knight Foundation, 2017, knightfoundation.org/public-media-white-paper-2017-ragusea

[203] CPB, "Overview Fact Sheet."

[204] CPB, "Preliminary FY 2019 Operating Budget," Corporation for Public Broadcasting, Accessed April 7, 2020, cpb.org/sites/default/files/Approved%20FY%202019%20Operating%20Budget.pdf

[205] CPB, "2020 Radio Community Service Grants General Provisions and Eligibility Criteria," Corporation for Public Broadcasting, October 2019, cpb.org/sites/default/files/stations/radio/generalprovisions/FY-2020-Radio-General-Provisions.pdf

[206] NPR, "Public Radio Finances," National Public Radio, Accessed April 7, 2020, npr.org/about-npr/178660742/public-radio-finances

[207] Victor Pickard, "Journalism's Failure," hbr.org/2020/03/journalisms-market-failure-is-a-crisis-for-democracy

208 CPB, "CPB Support for Rural Stations," Corporation for Public Broadcasting, Accessed April 7, 2020, cpb. org/aboutpb/rural

209 Current, "Our Guide to State Funding of Public Media," Current, Accessed April 7, 2020, current.org/ state-funding-guide

210 APM, "Organizational Structure," American Public Media, Accessed April 7, 2020, americanpublicmedia.org/about/org-structure

211 Ursula Ruedenberg (Pacifica Affiliate Network Manager) in correspondence with the author, April 1, 2020.

212 Bob Papper, "2019 Research: Local TV and Radio News Strengths," rtdna.org/article/2019_research_local_ tv_and_radio_news_strengths

213 FCC, "Nonprofit Media," Federal Communication Commission, Accessed April 7, 2020, transition.fcc.gov/ osp/inc-report/INoC-6-Public-Broadcasting.pdf

214 Kerri Hoffman, April 1, 2020

215 CPB, "Overview Fact Sheet," Corporation for Public Broadcasting, December 2019, cpb.org/sites/default/ files/CPB_Fact_Sheet.pdf

216 NPR, "Texas Public Radio Stations and NPR Launch Collaborative Statewide Newsroom," National Public Radio, September 5, 2019, npr.org/about-npr/759028569/texas-public-radio-stations-and-npr-launch-collaborative-statewide-newsroom

217 MWNB, "Mountain West News Bureau," KRCC, Southern Colorado NPR, Accessed April 8, 2020, krcc.org/ programs/mountain-west-news-bureau

218 NPR, "CPB, NPR Partner with Public Media Stations to Launch Gulf States Newsroom," National Public Radio, February 20, 2020, npr.org/about-npr/807704118/cpb-npr-partner-with-public-media-stations-to-launch-gulf-states-newsroom

219 Ibid

220 Chuck Holmes, executive director WBHM, in discussion with author, March 13, 2020

221 Elizabeth Jensen, "Working Together to Alleviate 'News Deserts,'" NPR Opinion, National Public Radio, March 6, 2020, npr.org/sections/publiceditor/2020/03/06/812096584/working-together-to-alleviate-news-deserts

222 Howard Husock, discussion with the author, March 13, 2020.

223 WAMU, "Homepage," WAMU, American University Radio, Accessed April 8, 2020, wamu.org

224 Julie Drizin,in correspondence with the author, March 17, 2020

225 Kerri Hoffman, April 1, 2020

226 Bob Papper, "2019 Research: Local TV and Radio News Strengths, rtdna.org/article/2019_research_local_ tv_and_radio_news_strengths

227 Steve Coll, "Reboot," CJR, Columbia Journalism Review, November/December 2010, archives.cjr.org/ cover_story/reboot.php

228 Vincent Stehle, "In the Covid-19 Crisis, Philanthropy's Investment in Local News Pays Off," The Chronicle of Philanthropy, March 26, 2020, philanthropy.com/article/In-the-Covid-19-Crisis/248347?cid=cpfd_home

229 Erik Wemple, "Stimulus Funding Can't Come Fast Enough for Public Broadcasters," Washington Post, ,

March 27, 2020, washingtonpost.com/opinions/2020/03/27/stimulus-funding-cant-come-fast-enough-public-broadcasters

[230] Gregg Re, "Senate Coronavirus Bill Includes $75M for Corporation for Public Broadcasting, Which Funds NPR, 'Big Bird,'" Fox News, March 25, 2020, foxnews.com/politics/senate-coronavirus-bill-75m-corporation-for-public-broadcasting-npr-big-bird

[231] William Tayman Jr., "Proposed FY 2020 Operating Budget," Corporation for Public Broadcasting, September 18, 2019, cpb.org/files/aboutcpb/financials/budget/FY2020-Operating-Budget.pdf

[232] WNYC, "Homepage," WNYC, New York Public Radio, Accessed April 8, 2020, wnyc.org

[233] Laura Walker (former president and CEO, WNYC) in discussion with the author, March 16, 2020

[234] Howard Husock , March 13, 2020

[235] Victor Pickard, "Journalism's Failure," hbr.org/2020/03/journalisms-market-failure-is-a-crisis-for-democracy

[236] Kerri Hoffman, "Public Radio Beyond the Pandemic," Medium, April 1, 2020, medium.com/prxofficial/public-radio-beyond-the-pandemic

[237] facebook.com/journalismproject/facebook-today-in-expands

[238] Phone interview, April 15, 2020

[239] Phone interview April 15, 2020

[240] pewresearch.org/fact-tank/2019/09/11/key-findings-about-the-online-news-landscape-in-america

[241] niemanlab.org/2019/01/facebook-is-committing-300-million-to-support-news-with-an-emphasis-on-local

[242] about.fb.com/news/2019/10/introducing-facebook-news

[243] hsjmc.umn.edu/news/2019-09-09-new-study-local-news-facebook

[244] UNC researchers took a random sample of 40 percent of the articles on the Today In app in major metro areas to produce a final sample of 1,103 articles, sourced by one of four categories: daily newspaper, non-daily newspaper, TV news, or other

[245] UNC researchers followed Today In apps for three North Carolina cities in September 2019 and April 2020: Chapel Hill (population 61,000), Durham (population 274,000) and Raleigh (population 469,000)

[246] facebook.com/journalismproject/facebook-research-news-deserts

[247] fcc.gov/news-events/blog/2012/07/25/review-literature-regarding-critical-information-needs-american-public

[248] Facebook followers were taken from Facebook pages on 11/22/2019. WRAL: 603,601 followers, ABC 11: 474,138 followers, CBS17: 158,813 followers, News & Observer -- 115,858 followers

[249] niemanlab.org/2019/09/researchers-analyzed-more-than-300000-local-news-stories-on-facebook-heres-what-they-found

[250] fcc.gov/news-events/blog/2012/07/25/review-literature-regarding-critical-information-needs-american-public

[251] niemanlab.org/2019/09/researchers-analyzed-more-than-300000-local-news-stories-on-facebook-heres-what-they-found

[252] localnewsinitiative.northwestern.edu/posts/2019/09/09/news-leaders-defender

[253] Phone interview April 16,2020

[254] about.fb.com/news/2019/10/introducing-facebook-news

255 Phone interview April 16, 2020

256 washingtonpost.com/lifestyle/media/the-future-of-local-newspapers-just-got-bleaker-heres-why-we-cant-let-them-die/2020/02/14/a7089d16-4f39-11ea-9b5c-eac5b16dafaa_story.html

257 Stephanie Sugars, "From fake news to enemy of the people: An anatomy of Trump's tweets," CPJ, January 30, 2019, cpj.org/2019/01/trump-twitter-press-fake-news-enemy-people

258 SBA, "Paycheck Protection Program," SBA, Accessed June 8, 2020, sba.gov/funding-programs/loans/coronavirus-relief-options/paycheck-protection-program#section-header-2

259 Keach Hagey, Jeffrey Trachtenberg, and Lindsay Wise, "Without Cornavirus Aid, Local Newspapers Could Fold," Wall Street Journal, April 27, 2020, wsj.com/articles/many-newspapers-want-coronavirus-stimulus-four-out-of-five-cant-get-it-11587987059

260 Jon Allsop, "The complications of federal assistance for newsrooms," Columbia Journalism Review, May 13, 2020, cjr.org/the_media_today/ppp_loans_government_funding_media.php

261 Letter from Maria Cantwell et al. to Mitch McConnell and Charles Schumer, April 18th, 2020, kennedy.senate.gov/public/_cache/files/d/e/de5c7999-e116-4fa7-b8a9-f0708fa98481/A4603E1DFFABCAFAB2274E07022378ED.2020-04-18-local-newspaper-broadcaster-letter-final.pdf

262 HEROES Act, May 15, 2020, docs.house.gov/billsthisweek/20200511/BILLS-116hr6800ih.pdf

263 See "Can Journalism Be Saved," New York Review of Books, February 27, 2020, interview with Nicholas Lemann

264 Tweet from Matt Pearce, April 30, 2020, twitter.com/mattdpearce/status/1255896227113168899

265 Letter from Debbie Dingell et al. to Donald Trump, April 20, 2020, upton.house.gov/uploadedfiles/200420supportlocalbroadcasters.pdf

266 Tim Ryan et al., "Congressman Tim Ryan Urges House Speaker Pelosi to Provide Assistance to Local Media Outlets and Journalists," Press Release, Office of Time Ryan, April 16, 2020, timryan.house.gov/media/press-releases/congressman-tim-ryan-urges-house-speaker-pelosi-provide-assistance-local-media

267 Ryan's press release shows support for four proposals: funding of public service ads, easing the transition to nonprofits, providing a tax credit for journalism jobs and offering newsrooms deferred interest loans. As of this writing, Ryan has not offered details. We comment on the first two ideas, which are supported by specific proposals

268 Steve Waldman, "Curing Local News for Good," Columbia Journalism Review, March 31, 2020, cjr.org/analysis/local-news-rescue-plan.php

269 News Media Alliance, "Support Local Media," News Media Alliance, Accessed June 8, 2020, newsmediaalliance.org/wp-content/uploads/2020/04/NEEDED-SUPPORT-FOR-LOCAL-MEDIA-FINAL.pdf

270 Corey Kilgannon, "A Community Newspaper Gets Tough on a Village. The Village Pulls Its Ads," New York Times, February 7, 2019, nytimes.com/2019/02/07/nyregion/garden-city-news-village-hall.html

271 Kevin G. Hall, "Federal agency says it will assume McClatchy pension plan if bankruptcy judge signs off," Impact 2020, May 13, 2020, mcclatchydc.com/news/nation-world/national/article242703376.html

272 American Benefits Council, "Groundbreaking Study of 703 Companies Reveals: Funding Rules will Divert Over $24 Billion from Economic Recovery in One Year," American Benefits Council, April 21, 2020, americanbenefitscouncil.org/pub/?id=8E337716-1866-DAAC-99FB-FE7DC3428BE4

273 Motley Fool Transcribers, "Gannett Co Inc (GCI) Q1 2020 Earnings Call Transcript," MFT, May 7, 2020, fool.com/earnings/call-transcripts/2020/05/07/gannett-co-inc-gci-q1-2020-earnings-call-transcrip.aspx

274 Take Responsibility for Workers and Families Act, March 22, 2020, napa-net.org/sites/napa-net.org/files/House-Democrats-Counterproposal-For-Stimulus.pdf

275 See endnote 115

276 CBO, "Save Community Newspaper Act of 2018 Cost Estimate," Congressional Budget Office, September 10, 2018, cbo.gov/system/files/2018-09/hr6377.pdf

277 Mike Lee, "Preventing Another Pension Bailout," Office of Mike Lee, November 8, 2019, lee.senate.gov/public/index.cfm/issue-in-focus?ID=B18A1CF4-ADD6-4034-8E33-BE26283505AA

278 According to the News Media Alliance, the HEROES Act's pension expansion would benefit McClatchy papers, the San Diego Tribune, the Keene Sentinel in New Hampshire and Vermont, Newspapers of New England, and the Daily Gazette in Schenectady, New York

279 Kevin G. Hall, "Federal agency says it will assume McClatchy pension plan if bankruptcy judge signs off," Impact 2020, May 13, 2020, mcclatchydc.com/news/nation-world/national/article242703376.html

280 Kristen Hare, "Here are the newsroom layoffs, furloughs and closures caused by the coronavirus," Poynter, June 5, 2020, poynter.org/business-work/2020/here-are-the-newsroom-layoffs-furloughs-and-closures-caused-by-the-coronavirus

281 Elizabeth Grieco, "U.S. newspapers have shed half of their newsroom employees since 2008," FactTank, Pew Research, April 20, 2020, pewresearch.org/fact-tank/2020/04/20/u-s-newsroom-employment-has-dropped-by-a-quarter-since-2008

282 Free Press Action, "What a Journalism-Recovery Package Should Look Like," Free Press Action, May 11, 2020, freepress.net/policy-library/what-journalism-recovery-package-should-look. See also: newsguild.org/wp-content/uploads/2020/04/TNG-CWA-letter-to-the-hill-April-9.pdf

283 Letter from Tim Ryan to Nancy Pelosi, April, 2020. dearcolleague.us/2020/04/letter-to-leadership-to-protect-local-media-in-next-coronavirus-package-2

284 HEROES Act, Section 20211. The credit was created by the CARES Act, section 2301congress.gov/bill/116th-congress/house-bill/6800/text; congress.gov/bill/116th-congress/house-bill/748/text?format=txt

285 Mitt Romney, "Romney "Patriot Pay" Plan Would Support America's Frontline Workers," Office of Mitt Romney, May 1, 2020, romney.senate.gov/romney-patriot-pay-plan-would-support-americas-frontline-workers

286 Steve Waldman, "Curing Local News for Good," Columbia Journalism Review, March 31, 2020, cjr.org/analysis/local-news-rescue-plan.php

287 H.R.3226 – Saving Local News Act of 2019, congress.gov/bill/116th-congress/house-bill/3126?q=%7B%22search%22%3A%5B%22savin

288 documentcloud.org/documents/6549394-SaltLakeTribuneIRS.html#document/p25

289 David Schizer, "Subsidizing the Press," Journal of Legal Analysis, Vol 3 no. 1, Spring 2011, academic.oup.com/jla/article/3/1/1/857941

290 Interview with David Schizer

291 Benjamin Mullin, "NPR Chief Warns of Steep Cost Cuts Amid Coronavirus Pandemic," Wall Street Journal, April 16, 2020, wsj.com/articles/npr-chief-warns-of-steep-cost-cuts-amid-coronavirus-pandemic-11587093462

292 The author was employed at CPB when political interference was attempted and rebuffed

293 Free Press Action, "What a Journalism-Recovery Package Should Look Like," Free Press Action, May 11, 2020, freepress.net/policy-library/what-journalism-recovery-package-should-look

294 Steve Waldman, "Curing Local News for Good," Columbia Journalism Review, March 31, 2020, cjr.org/analysis/local-news-rescue-plan.php

295 washingtonpost.com/posteverything/wp/2017/03/17/public-broadcast-has-outlived-its-mandate-time-to-justify-its-government-subsidy

296 cpb.org/aboutcpb/history-timeline

297 congress.gov/116/bills/hr1865/BILLS-116hr1865enr.pdf

298 Interview with Robert Papper, Radio Television Digital News Association/Hofstra University Newsroom Survey

299 Ibid.

300 nationalaffairs.com/publications/detail/a-new-role-for-public-broadcasting, and Interview with Howard Husock

301 Pew Research Center, "An overwhelming majority of Americans get at least some local news online," Pew Research Center, March 19, 2019, journalism.org/2019/03/26/nearly-as-many-americans-prefer-to-get-their-local-news-online-as-prefer-the-tv-set/pj_2019-03-26_local-news_1-02

302 Douglas Clark, "US Digital Ad Spending Will Surpass Traditional in 2019," emarketer, February 20, 2019, newsroom.emarketer.com/newsroom/index.php/us-digital-ad-spending-will-surpass-traditional-in-2019

303 Ibid

304 Ibid

305 newsmediaalliance.org/release-new-study-google-revenue-from-news-publishers-content

306 newsmediaalliance.org/statement-do-publishers-really-keep-70-of-ad-revenue-tech-spox-says-yes-publishers-disagree

307 newsmediaalliance.org/statement-do-publishers-really-keep-70-of-ad-revenue-tech-spox-says-yes-publishers-disagree/. For the tech perspective, see Ben Smith's analysis: stratechery.com/2020/media-regulators-and-big-tech-indulgences-and-injunctions-better-approaches

308 congress.gov/bill/116th-congress/house-bill/2054/text?q=%7B%22search%22%3A%5B%22Hr+2054%22%5D%7D

309 congress.gov/bill/116th-congress/senate-bill/1700?q=%7B%22search%22%3A%5B%22journalism+competition+and+preservation+act%22%5D%7D&s=1&r=

310 As a presidential candidate, Bernie Sanders said his administration would explore new ways to empower media organizations to collectively bargain with tech monopolies, but he has yet to sign on to the bill

311 Conversation with Danielle Coffey, News Media Alliance

312 knightfoundation.org/wp-content/uploads/2020/03/Gallup-Knight-Report-Techlash-Americas-Growing-Concern-with-Major-Tech-Companies-Final.pdf

313 wsj.com/articles/justice-department-ramps-up-google-probe-with-heavy-focus-on-ad-tools-11580904003. See also: cnbc.com/2020/02/11/ftc-will-examine-prior-acquisitions-by-big-tech-companies.html, and: washingtonpost.com/technology/2019/10/07/roughly-state-attorneys-general-plan-take-part-facebook-antitrust-probe-sources-say

314 wsj.com/articles/justice-department-state-attorneys-general-likely-to-bring-antitrust-lawsuits-against-

google-11589573622

315 nytimes.com/2020/04/20/business/media/australia-facebook-google.html

316 reuters.com/article/us-tech-antitrust/house-antitrust-probe-report-likely-by-first-part-of-2020-idUSKBN1WX1WA

317 Conversation with Cicilline's office

318 niemanlab.org/2020/01/dont-expect-mcconnells-paradox-to-help-news-publishers-get-real-money-out-of-google-and-facebook/?relatedstory

319 niemanlab.org/2020/05/newsonomics-how-will-the-pandemic-panic-reshape-the-local-news-industry

320 twitter.com/benyt/status/1255964149210808331?lang=en

321 Papper interview

322 rtdna.org/uploads/files/2018%20Local%20News%20Research.pdf

323 nytimes.com/2017/11/09/opinion/ajit-pai-media-ownership.html

324 archives.cjr.org/essay/from_the_desk_of_a_former_fcc.php, Copp interview

325 nytimes.com/2018/04/02/business/media/sinclair-news-anchors-script.html

326 supremecourt.gov/DocketPDF/19/19-1231/141900/20200417141044916_OSG%20Prometheus%20Cert%20Petition%2014.pdf

327 supremecourt.gov/DocketPDF/19/19-1241/142112/20200421095240271_Prometheus%20Corrected%20Petition.pdf

328 niemanlab.org/2020/05/newsonomics-how-will-the-pandemic-panic-reshape-the-local-news-industry/

329 HR 1789, Local and Independent Television Protection Act of 2019.

330 The commission proposed an incubator program, but it's now blocked in court with the FCC's other 2017 rule changes. The program encouraged established stations to provide financial or management to aspiring stations. Mentor stations would then receive a "reward waiver," enabling them to skirt ownership limits. Democratic Commissioner Jessica Rosenworcel opposed the program, worrying it would promote consolidation

331 H.R. 3957, the Expanding Broadcast Ownership Opportunities Act of 2017

332 Remarks of Commissioner Geoffrey Starks before the National Association of Broadcasters Board of Directors, Miami, FL, January 27, 2020, energycommerce.house.gov/sites/democrats.energycommerce.house.gov/files/documents/2020.01.15_Briefing%20Memo%20CAT%20Leg%20Hearing%20-%20Diversity%20in%20Media%20Ownership.pdf

333 Adarand v Peña, oyez.org/cases/1994/93-1841

334 From remarks of FCC Commissioner Geoffrey Starks before the National Association Board of Directors, January 27, 2020

335 congress.gov/bill/116th-congress/house-bill/5567?q=%7B%22search%22%3A%5B%22hr+5567%22%5D%7D&s=2&r=1

336 For more discussion see newspaperownership.com/wp-content/uploads/2016/09/07.UNC_RiseOfNewMediaBaron_SinglePage_01Sep2016-REDUCED.pdf

337 democrats.senate.gov/newsroom/press-releases/schumer-demands-new-information-from-alden-

global-capital-hedge-fund-known-for-destroying-local-newspapers-and-slashing-jobs-across-the-country-regarding-their-efforts-to-acquire-gannett-and-the-potential-free-speech-and-pension-stability-implications-of-such-a-takeover

338 durbin.senate.gov/imo/media/doc/Letter%20to%20Alden%20Global%20Capital%20FINAL.pdf.

339 poynter.org/business-work/2020/its-time-to-uproot-american-newspapers-from-hedge-funds-and-replant-them-into-more-hospitable-ground

340 warren.senate.gov/imo/media/doc/2019.7.17%20Stop%20Wall%20Street%20Looting%20Act%20Analysis.pdf

341 Interview with Eileen Appelbaum

342 Wall Street Journal, Chamber of Commerce Joins Pushback Against Warren's Private-Equity Plan

343 news.bloomberglaw.com/bloomberg-law-analysis/analysis-private-equity-firms-should-fear-warrens-looting-act

344 freepress.net/our-response/expert-analysis/insights-opinions/why-civic-info-consortium-such-huge-deal

345 A breakdown of NJ's $920M in frozen spending, BridgeTower Media, April 16, 2020

346 ncsl.org/research/fiscal-policy/coronavirus-covid-19-state-budget-updates-and-revenue-projections637208306.aspx

347 Center on Budget and Policy Priorities, States Grappling with Hit to Tax Collections

348 Margaret Sullivan, "The Local News Crisis is Destroying What a Divided America Desperately Needs: Common Ground," The Washington Post, August 5, 2018

washingtonpost.com/lifestyle/style/the-local-news-crisis-is-destroying-what-a-divided-america-desperately-needs-common-ground/2018/08/03/d654d5a8-9711-11e8-810c-5fa705927d54_story.html

349 Transcript of Mark Zuckerberg's testimony before the Senate Judicial and Commerce Committees, April 10, 2018. judiciary.senate.gov/imo/media/doc/04-10-18%20Zuckerberg%20Testimony.pdf

350 Victor Pickard, Democracy without Journalism: confronting the misinformation society, (Oxford University Press, 2020)

352 Duke University: Jessica Mahone et al. "Who's Producing Local Journalism" (August 2019); and Philip Napoli et al. "Assessing Local Journalism: News Deserts, Journalism Divides and the Determinants of Local News (August 2018)

353 UNC: Penelope Abernathy et al. "The Algorithm as Editor" in News Deserts and Ghost Newspapers: Will Local News Survive? (May 2020); and Justin Blankenship. "What Makes the News? TV's Coverage of Rural Communities" in Thwarting the Emergence of News Deserts (March 2017)

354 University of Minnesota: Matt Weber et al. "Local News on Facebook: Assessing the Critical Information Needs Served Through Facebook's Today In Feature." (September 2019)

METHODOLOGY

The findings in this report are based on information in a comprehensive proprietary database that is created and maintained by the Center for Innovation and Sustainability in Local Media at the University of North Carolina at Chapel Hill. Over the past six years, faculty and researchers in the Hussman School of Journalism and Media collected data on more than 9,000 local newspapers, 1,400 public broadcasting outlets, 950 ethnic media and 525 digital sites. The information is derived from a variety of industry and government sources, supplemented with extensive research and reporting, fact-checking and multiple layers of verification. UNC maintains six separate databases on newspapers that were published in 2004, 2014, 2016, 2017, 2018 and 2019, plus two databases on local digital sites published in 2018 and 2020. With the 2020 report, we are also creating two new databases with information on ethnic media and public broadcasting outlets.

Our first two databases (of newspapers published in 2004 and 2014) were created in 2014, as an effort to track the fate of the country's local newspapers over the previous decade, a tumultuous period in the industry. Extensive research has concluded that local newspapers have historically been the prime source of news and information that guides decision-making of residents and government officials at the grassroots level on issues such as education, elections and the environment (to name but a few). So, we focused first on finding data on the thousands of small dailies and weeklies in this country, since there was no comprehensive and reliable source of information on them. Our 2016 report tracked the loss of local newspapers. Our 2018 and 2020 reports added a new layer of research as we sought to assess the health of the news ecosystem in a community. In 2018, we added information on local digital sites, and with this 2020 report, we are compiling our first list of ethnic media and public broadcasting outlets.

- **Newspapers:** Information on individual newspapers in the database has been cross-referenced with at least four sources. Our database was initially created using statistics gleaned from two industry databases: Editor & Publisher DataBook (published 2004–2017) and E&P data accessed online for the years 2016–2019, as well as proprietary information collected and provided by the consulting firm BIA/Kelsey for the years 2004 and 2014. Researchers then verified these data with information obtained from 55 state, regional and national press associations, and our own extensive independent online research, ascertaining the content of newspapers by checking websites and print versions, and also interviewing editors and publishers when appropriate.

- **Local News Sites:** Our list of local news sites was compiled by merging lists provided by the Local Independent Online News (LION) organization, the Institute for Nonprofit News (INN) and the Google-sponsored Project Oasis. As with newspapers, researchers then visited all of the websites to verify that the content was updated regularly and that the domain was still active.

- **Ethnic news outlets:** Our list of ethnic media outlets in the United States was compiled and cross-referenced, using lists of ethnic newspapers in the Editor & Publisher DataBook (2004 and 2018), the Craig Newmark School of Journalism's (CUNY) State of Latino News Media, the National Newspaper Publishers Association (NNPA, an association of African American newspapers) and the National Association of Black Owned Broadcasters (NABOB).

- **Public broadcasting outlets:** The list of public radio and television stations came from data supplied by Public Broadcasting Service (PBS), National Public Radio (NPR), American Public Media (APM) and Pacifica. To determine if a station produced original content, we reviewed individual station's schedules and contacted individual stations with questions.

In addition, we used media information in the report contained in numerous surveys and reports by, among others, the Knight Commission on Trust in Media and Democracy, the Gallup organization, and the Pew Research Center.

Layers of demographic, political and economic data from government sources were also added to the database. By visiting this website – usnewsdeserts.com – and using the interactive maps, researchers, as well as interested citizens, can drill down to the county level in all 50 states and compare how communities across the country have been affected by the closing of local newspapers.

Despite adding multiple layers of verification, we realize the UNC Database is still prone to errors inherent in any large database, particularly one that depends in part on surveys and the accurate feedback of respondents. When we spot errors, we correct them in the database and will continue to update our analysis as new information becomes available. If you detect an error, please fill in and submit the corrections form available on our website. In general, we attempt to update our most current year's database on a quarterly basis.

Since these are some of the most comprehensive and up-to-date databases on news organizations, we make every effort to share them with serious academic and industry researchers who are pursuing related or relevant topics. If you would like access to our databases of news organizations, please click here to fill out a request form.

Building and Refining the Newspaper Database

By surveying all 50 state press associations in 2017 and 2018, we identified 300 local newspapers that existed in 2004 but were not listed in national industry databases. Therefore, in our 2018 report, we adjusted upward the number of newspapers in our 2004 database – to 8,891 newspapers (1,472 daily; 7,419 weekly). Our 2020 report keys off the revised numbers for 2004 in our 2018 report. Our 2020 report identifies 6,734 local newspapers in the country – 1,260 dailies and 5,474 weeklies – that were still being published at the end of 2019. Each newspaper in the database has the following variables: year, name, frequency (daily/weekly), number of days published per week, city, state, parent media company and total circulation.

Our research is concerned with identifying local newspapers that provide public-service journalism. Therefore, in addition to using industry and press association lists, we add a fourth layer of verification. We consult both online and print editions of newspapers, analyzing the content of several editions of a paper, asking the following questions. Does the paper, for example, cover local government meetings, such as school boards and county commissioner meetings? Does the paper provide coverage on any of the eight topics identified by the Federal Communications Commission as being "critical information needs"?

Intentionally excluded from our proprietary database are shoppers, community newsletters (which focus on people and events, instead of news), specialty publications (such as business journals and lifestyle magazines), monthly and bimonthly publications, advertising inserts, TMCs (Total Market Coverage publications), and some zoned editions that feature minimal local journalism relevant to the county where the zoned edition circulates. This report assesses the quantity, but not the quality of news generated by local news outlets, a step that would require in-depth analysis of the content. We recommend this as an additional research step to anyone seeking to determine the health of the local news ecosystem in a specific region.

Many states and municipalities have different thresholds for determining if a newspaper is a "paper of record" and therefore eligible to carry legal advertisements. Often that threshold is based on circulation and distribution. We recognize that the income from legal advertising is very critical to small dailies and weeklies. Therefore, we can work with the general counsel at individual press associations to provide qualifying text on state maps that explain the difference in our methodology (which is focused on news coverage) versus the threshold used by government officials to determine if a publication is eligible to receive legal advertising. The counsel for state press associations should contact us with requests for qualifying text concerning the status of publications that meet the threshold for legal advertising.

Defining "News Deserts" and "Ghost Newspapers"

As a result of our extra layers of verification, we expanded our definition of "news deserts" and introduced the concept of "ghost newspapers" in our 2018 report. Previously, we defined a news desert as a community without a newspaper. As a result of the dramatic shrinkage in the number of local news outlets in recent years – without alternative news media to replace them – we have expanded our definition of news deserts to include communities where residents are facing significantly diminished access to the sort of important local news and information that feeds grassroots democracy.

We also noted that a number of traditional stand-alone newspapers had become shells, or "ghosts," of their former selves. They are no longer providing residents with the news they need to make informed decisions about a range of important issues that could affect their quality of life. We identified two types of ghost newspapers: the once-iconic weeklies that merged with larger dailies and evolved into shoppers or specialty publications, and the metro and regional state papers that have dramatically scaled back their newsroom staffing, as well as their government coverage of inner-city, suburban and rural communities.

UNC removed from the 2018 database almost 600 weeklies that were stand-alone traditional newspapers in 2004, but by 2018 had evolved into shoppers, advertising supplements or specialty publications such as lifestyle magazines or business journals. We did not remove the larger metro and regional state papers, but estimated the number – at least 1,000 – by comparing industry statistics on newsroom staffing and circulation to news articles about the size of an individual paper's newsroom staffing in 2004 compared with 2018. To determine definitively whether a large daily is fulfilling its civic journalism role of informing a community on important issues, much more research – including in-depth analysis of published content – is needed. Having raised the issue, we leave that to other researchers to determine whether an individual paper is a "ghost."

As was the case with the 2016 report, because our focus is on local newspapers, UNC also excluded from the 2018 and 2020 reports data on the country's largest national papers – The New York Times, The Wall Street Journal and USA Today – as well as shoppers, magazines and other specialty publications. In total, 2,196 papers that were closed, merged or morphed into shoppers or specialty publications over the past 15 years were removed from the UNC database to arrive at the 2019 number. Nevertheless, the 2020 tally of 6,734 papers may overstate the number of stand-alone newspapers. Based on UNC's analysis of papers owned by the largest 25 chains, an estimated 10 to 15 percent of newspapers still listed in industry databases may be, in fact, zoned editions of larger papers. Nevertheless, these zoned editions were not removed from the 2018 tally, since they are still providing news coverage of important events and issues in their communities.

Dealing with Circulation Limitations

There is currently no widely accepted and easily accessible tracking system of online readership data, especially for the thousands of local papers in small and mid-sized markets. Therefore, print circulation is used as a proxy for measuring the decline in both the reach and influence of traditional newspapers.

The print circulation figures in our database come with limitations. Some circulation figures are audited and verified; others are self-reported. Therefore, in our 2018 database, we've added additional verification steps and information in an attempt to be as transparent as possible about where we are getting the numbers. We also noted whether the reported circulation is free or paid circulation.

When possible, we use circulation numbers from the Alliance for Audited Media (AAM). AAM is the industry leader in media verification and specializes in verifying circulation metrics for publishers. However, only 13 percent of papers in the UNC Database subscribe to AAM audits. Additionally, the reported AAM numbers for the large dailies often lag behind the audit by a couple of years.

Because news organizations must pay AAM to verify their circulation statistics, many small papers do not use the service and instead self-report. If there are no AAM data, UNC relied on self-reported newspaper circulation from a variety of sources (E&P, state press associations and independent research). Self-reported circulation data are problematic, since UNC researchers observed that a significant number of newspapers report the same circulation across multiple years. However, self-reported numbers are the only option available for many small weekly papers.

U.S. and State Maps

For the 2018 and 2020 report, UNC created interactive maps for the country and all 50 states, plus the District of Columbia. The maps in this report, and in its online version, provide insights into the risk of news deserts in thousands of communities across the country. By visitingusnewsdeserts.com, researchers can analyze data (demographics, political leanings, number of news outlets) down to the county level for all 50 states. UNC researchers used government data to pinpoint the locations of newspapers as accurately as possible. Often, both the BIA/Kelsey and E&P 2014 databases incorrectly listed the parent company or city location for many newspapers, especially the smaller ones. UNC researchers attempted to review and correct errors. The UNC Database uses the newspaper's office as the physical address for mapping purposes.

To identify whether newspapers were located in a rural or an urban area, each was assigned to a corresponding group from the U.S. Department of Agriculture's Rural-Urban Continuum Codes (RUCC) based on the county in which they were located. According to RUCC codes, communities in groups one through three were classified as metro areas. All others were classified as rural. Additionally, U.S. Census information on demographics (income, age, population makeup, etc.) was merged into the databases, as well as information from state election boards and industry sources such as the Local Independent Online News (LION) association. We also overlaid the USDA's information to locate counties in food deserts. The USDA defines a food desert as "parts of the country vapid of fresh fruit, vegetables, and other healthful whole foods, usually found in impoverished areas due to a lack of grocery stores, farmers' markets and healthy food providers."

For national and state maps, click here.

Tracking Sales, Mergers and Closures

UNC tracks changes in a newspaper's ownership, as well as closures and mergers, through news accounts and press releases. We define a closure as a newspaper that is no longer published and a merger as a newspaper that has been combined with another publication. Often the two merged papers initially have a combined name, but eventually the name of the smaller paper is eliminated. We tracked mergers and acquisitions in the newspaper industry from 2004 to 2020 and assessed corporate strategies by identifying and examining:

Publicly available corporate documents, including quarterly and annual reports released by the individual companies and press releases by Dirks, Van Essen, Murray & April and by Cribb, Greene & Cope, two of the leading merger and acquisition firms in the U.S. newspaper industry.

- Numerous news articles about individual purchases and business decisions.
- Statements made by executives that were in press releases, news articles or industry presentations.
- Reports and interviews with industry representatives and analysts.

There are limitations to all of the above sources. Press releases, news articles, statements made by news executives and reports from industry analysts often list by title only the sales of the largest and most prominent newspapers, usually dailies. The weeklies involved in the sale, as well as specialty publications (including shoppers and business journals) are often grouped together and reported as a single number. That is why we try to check all announcements of sales against publicly available documents and corporate websites.

We track updates to the industry through the Twitter account @businessofnews and post important developments on our website here. For the past three years, we've attempted to update the current year's database on a quarterly basis. The final update of the 2019 database occurred in January 2020, when all transactions that occurred in the fourth quarter of the previous year were recorded.

Media Groupings

Similar to our 2016 and 2018 reports, UNC categorized the largest 25 newspaper owners into one of three categories: private companies, publicly traded companies and investment companies.

- **Private Companies:** This group includes large companies, such as Hearst Corp., which own a portfolio of media that include an array of media formats. They not only own print publications, but cable networks and digital enterprises as well. This category can also include smaller companies like Boone Newspapers, which owns fewer than 100 publications in small and mid-sized communities throughout the South.

- **Public Companies:** This group includes publicly traded companies such as Gannett, Lee Enterprises and McClatchy.

- **Investment Companies:** This category has arisen in the past decade and has a different ownership philosophy and financial structure from the traditional newspaper owners. Owners in this group can be either private or public, but the key distinctions in investment company ownership are the companies' business philosophies and financial structures, which differ significantly from those of traditional newspaper chains. Companies were classified in this category if they met at least five of the eight characteristics in the chart below:

HOW INVESTMENT COMPANIES DIFFER FROM TRADITIONAL NEWSPAPER CHAINS

CHARACTERISTICS	NewMedia/ GateHouse	Digital First	CNHI	Civitas	tronc/ Tribune	BH Media	10/13 Communications
The stated emphasis of the parent company is to maximize shareholder return on investment.	X	X	X	X	X	X	X
Many properties were acquired as a group from other media companies through either purchase of entire companies or divisions.	X	X	X	X	X	X	X
Majority financial and/or operational control of the firm is held by a small number of institutional shareholders, such as lenders, private equity firms or investment fund managers.	X	X	X	X	X	X	X
The company was formed or incorporated within the past two decades and is a relative newcomer to newspaper ownership.	X	X	X	X		X	X
The newspaper holdings are part of a portfolio of non-newspaper companies.	X	X	X	X		X	X
There has been much movement of individual newspapers within portfolios.	X	X	X	X	X		
There have been two or more financial restructurings, including bankruptcy reorganization, a rebranding after selling the company or flips between public and private ownership.	X	X		X	X		
A private equity company, a hedge fund or pension fund has at some point during the past decade owned all or a significant portion of the enterprise.	X	X	X	X	X		X

SOURCE: UNC DATABASE

In the 2020 report, we note that investment companies – such as Gatehouse, Digital First and BH Media – are merging with the few remaining publicly traded companies, such as Gannett and Lee Enterprises, and forming mega-chains, once again altering the news landscape.

Facebook Data

In March 2019 Facebook shared data with four universities – Duke University, Harvard University, the University of Minnesota and the University of North Carolina at Chapel Hill – on its "Today In" platform, which provides links to articles from local news organizations. To get an idea of the quality of information in the news articles available to North Carolina residents, the UNC team of four researchers focused on the content of the "Today In" stories for the month of February 2019. Our analysis zeroed in on six major metropolitan areas in North Carolina, as determined by the Office of State Budget and Management. By cross-referencing the six major metropolitan areas in North Carolina and the cities that had the "Today In" app at the time, we created a list of 14 counties and 12 "Today In" cities for the analysis. The researchers coded and categorized "Today In" news articles in these cities as to whether they provided users with public service journalism and information about the eight critical information needs (such as transportation, politics and education), as identified by the Federal Communications Commission. In addition, another researcher followed up by tracking the "Today In" news articles available to residents living in three cities in the Research Triangle area – Raleigh, Durham and Chapel Hill – during one week in September 2019.

About the Industry Databases

Newspapers and Digital Sites: Editor & Publisher began publishing an annual Newspaper DataBook in 1921. The DataBook has information on more than 25,000 companies and more than 160 data fields. Data are collected through mail and email surveys. BIA/Kelsey, a research and advisory company, focused on local advertising and marketing, began tracking newspaper ownership in 2004. The organization employs a telemarketing team that calls individual newspapers and collects information from employee respondents. Data on local digital sites were compiled from two separate lists maintained by the Local Independent Online News (LION) organization, the Institute for Nonprofit News (INN), and the Google-funded Project Oasis.

Ethnic Media: E&P provided data on three categories of ethnic newspapers: African American, Hispanic and Other. Through additional research, we were able to obtain data on the following ethnic newspapers: African American, Asian American, Latino, Native American and Other (including Polish, Russian and Armenian). This was supplemented with the data published by the City University of New York's Craig Newmark Graduate School of Journalism on "The State of the Latino News Media," published in June 2019. This report provided information on broadcast outlets and digital sites, as well newspapers. Additional information on African American media was obtained from the National Newspaper Publishers Association (NNPA) and the National Association of Black Owned Broadcasters (NABOB).

Public Broadcasting Outlets: Information on Public Broadcasting Stations comes from a map of member stations published by PBS on May 2018, referencing it with membership data from American Public Television Stations, a nonprofit organization of public television stations. National Public Radio (NPR) provided a list of members station, which was compared with the NPR's Station Finder Map. Information on American Public Media (APM) was derived from information on two sites, Southern California Public Radio and Minnesota Public Radio. Pacifica radio has an affiliate network of about 200 stations. However, after speaking with Director Ursula Ruedenberg, we included in our database the only four stations that produce original content: KPFA (Berkeley, California), KPFK (Los Angeles), WPFW (Washington, D.C.) and KPFT (Houston).

OTHER RESOURCES

Reports

This is the fourth report on the loss of local news, written and/or edited by Penelope Muse Abernathy, Knight Chair in Journalism and Digital Media Economics at the UNC Hussman School of Journalism and Media. Previous reports are listed below. All reports are available for downloading at: usnewsdeserts.com.

The Expanding News Desert (2018): The report analyzes the social, political and economic consequences posed by the rise of news deserts by documenting the loss of local newspapers in recent years and attempts by other media – including television and digital outlets – to fill the void. It also explores the indelible mark left on the newspaper industry by the financiers – hedge funds and private equity firms – who own and operate some of the largest chains in the country.

Thwarting the Emergence of News Deserts (2017): This edited collection of curated and invited articles provides insight into the topics discussed at a symposium at the Newseum in Washington, D.C., sponsored by the Knight Foundation and the UNC Hussman School of Journalism and Media. Each article offers a slightly different perspective on the possibilities and obstacles newspapers and communities across the country are confronting in the digital era. Two of the articles examine how ownership of five local newspapers in eastern North Carolina influenced coverage of the 2016 elections and the devastating aftermath of Hurricane Matthew.

The Rise of a New Media Baron and the Emerging Threat of News Deserts (2016): In the wake of the 2008 recession, a new type of media baron – private equity firms, hedge funds and other investment partnerships – swooped in to buy hundreds of distressed newspapers. These new owners prioritized bottom-line performance over journalism's civic mission. Their rise coincided with a period of immense disruption in the industry. This report documents the dramatic ownership trends during a pivotal decade (2004 to 2014) and considers the long-term implications for local news.

Books

In addition, the author has produced two books that explore for-profit and nonprofit business strategies for reviving local news.

The Strategic Digital Media Entrepreneur (Wiley Blackwell: 2018): Co-authored by two veteran media executives who are now university professors, the book offers a detailed compendium of lessons and case studies that identify emerging business models for both start-up and legacy companies attempting to craft strategies that take advantage of the interactive, always-on internet. Its companion website – cislm.org/digitalstrategy – has videos and additional case studies on entrepreneurial endeavors.

Saving Community Journalism: The Path to Profitability (UNC Press: 2014): This book acknowledges the civic contribution of a strong local newspaper while also exploring the economic peril many face. Examining experiences at a wide variety of community papers, it lays out a strategic path forward that leads to transformation and long-term economic sustainability. The companion website – savingcommunityjournalism.com – provides examples of how newspapers can shed legacy costs, rebuild a vibrant community on many platforms, and create new revenue opportunities.

CONTRIBUTORS

News Deserts and Ghost Newspapers: Will Local News Survive? and the website, usnewsdeserts.com, was produced by the Center for Innovation and Sustainability in Local Media in the Hussman School of Journalism and Media at the University of North Carolina at Chapel Hill.

About the Author and Editor

Penelope Muse Abernathy, formerly an executive at The Wall Street Journal and The New York Times, is the Knight Chair in Journalism and Digital Media Economics. She is author of two books on digital strategies for news organizations and four national reports on the state of local news.

About the Center

 UNC's Center for Innovation and Sustainability in Local Media supports existing and start-up news organizations through its dissemination of applied research and the development of digital tools and solutions. The Center, funded by the John S. and James L. Knight Foundation, supports the economic and business research of UNC's Knight Chair in Journalism and Digital Media Economics, as well as faculty and students in the design, testing and adaptation of digital tools and strategies for use in newsrooms.

Researchers

Bill Arthur, Senior Researcher and Writer

Dana Miller Ervin, Senior Researcher and Writer

Alex Dixon, Research Assistant

Jill Fontaine, Research Specialist

Zachary Metzger, Research Specialist '23 (Ph.D.)

Jeremiah Murphy, Research Specialist '20 (M.A.)

Student Researchers include:

Justin Kavlie '21 (Ph.D.), Lindsey Slack '21 (M.A.), Maydha Devarajan '22, Preston Fore '23, Praveena Somasundaram '22, Madison Wiedeman, '22, Alice Lim '21, Will Hausen '20, Mark Morrison '20, Ian McDaniel '19, Natasha Townsend '19

Other Significant Contributors

Michael McElroy, Project Manager and Adjunct Professor of Journalism

Sterling (Sting) Ching, Web and Design Project Manager

Leonardo Castaneda, Data Visualization Specialist

Stephanie Willen Brown, Director, Park Library

David Ardia, Associate Professor of Law, Co-Director of Center for Media Law and Policy

Bill Cloud, Associate Professor of Journalism (Ret.)

Angelia Herrin, Lecturer in Journalism

Blair Gosney, Outreach and Programs Coordinator

Yvette Thompson, Administrative Assistant

UNC Hussman School of Journalism and Media

Susan R. King, Dean

Louise Spieler, Senior Associate Dean

Susan Leath, Director, Center for Innovation and Sustainability in Local Media

CPSIA information can be obtained
at www.ICGtesting.com
Printed in the USA
LVHW071530270123
738013LV00023B/1545